Bookkeeping and Accounting Test for International Communication

# BATIC®

## 国際会計検定【バティック】

### 国際会計理論
## 公式問題集

### Sub.2

発行所／東京商工会議所
発売元／中央経済社

# 本書の特徴と使い方

　本書は、東京商工会議所が主催する「BATIC(国際会計検定)」対策の問題集です。「問題編」と「解答編」で構成されており、各Chapterの内容は「BATIC Subject2公式テキスト」に対応しています。

　問題編はマークシートでの解答に対応した選択式の問題と記述式の問題で構成されています。

　解答編では解答の他、和訳と簡単な解説がついていますので、単に正解の確認にとどまらず、理解を深めてください。

　巻末には、2019年に出題された試験問題を収録しました。検定試験同様に、時間を計りながら解くなど、受験前の腕試しにご活用ください。

## 〈解答にあたって〉

• 設問中に登場する企業の会計年度は、特に指示がない場合は暦年(1月1日から12月31日)として解答してください。

• 税率の表示および税額に関する指示がある場合のみ、税金を考慮して解答してください。

• 本書は2020年1月1日現在有効に成立している国際財務報告基準(IFRS)に準拠しています。

# 検定試験のご案内

BATIC（国際会計検定）®

Bookkeeping & Accounting Test for International Communication

## ■主催団体

東京商工会議所・施行商工会議所

## ■試験日

7月・12月

## ■申込方法・受験料

詳細はホームページ（https://www.kentei.org/）またはお電話（03-3989-0777）にてご確認ください。

## ■科目・配点

Subject1（英 文 簿 記）：400点　全受験者必須とする

Subject2（国際会計理論）：600点　受験者の習得レベルに応じて任意

合計1,000点

## ■受験資格

(1) Subject1（英文簿記）

なし

(2) Subject2（国際会計理論）

Accountant level（320点以上）取得者とする。

＊ Subject1・2の同時受験は可能ですが、Subject1がAccountant level（320点以上）に達しなかった場合は、Subject2の得点は認定されません。また、Accountant levelに達した場合は、Subject2の得点に400点を加算した点数が認定得点となります。

## ■試験時間

Subject1（英 文 簿 記）：1時間30分

Subject2（国際会計理論）：2時間30分

| | スコア<br>（1000 点満点） | 称号 | 概要 | 難易度<br>目安 |
|---|---|---|---|---|
| Subject<br>2 | 880 点以上 | Controller level<br>（コントローラーレベル） | 国際会計理論と国際的基準（国際財務報告基準〈IFRS〉）を理解し、国際的基準での財務諸表の作成、分析及び国内基準からの組替えができる。会計手続き、会計方針の策定とその推進ができる。 | 日商簿記<br>1 級程度 |
| | 700 点以上 | Accounting Manager level<br>（アカウンティング マネジャー<br>レベル） | 国際会計理論と国際的基準の基本的な部分を理解している。月次及び年度の会計報告ができる。適切な決算修正仕訳、精算表、基本的な財務諸表の作成ができる。 | 日商簿記<br>2 級程度 |
| Subject<br>1 | 320 点以上 | Accountant level<br>（アカウンタントレベル） | ブックキーパーに対する簡単な指示、英語による会計帳簿の記帳及び管理ができる。 | 日商簿記<br>3 級程度 |
| | 200 点以上 | Bookkeeper level<br>（ブックキーパーレベル） | 基本的な会計取引を理解できる。 | |
| | 200 点未満 | なし | Subject1 の得点が 200 点未満の場合は称号が付与されず、得点のみの認定となります。 | |

## ■出題方法

マークシート方式による選択問題と記述問題

## ■認定期間

「Accounting Manager level」および「Controller level」の認定期間は3年です。なお、「Bookkeeper level」および「Accountant level」には認定期間はありません。

# ■試験範囲

## 1. Bookkeeper Level & Accountant Level（配点 400 点）

| | |
|---|---|
| Basic Concepts of Accounting and Bookkeeping | 会計と簿記の基本概念 |
| Transactions and Journal Entries | 取引と仕訳 |
| Journal and Ledger | 仕訳帳と元帳 |
| Trial Balance | 試算表 |
| Adjusting Entries | 決算修正仕訳 |
| Accounting for Inventory and Cost of Sales | 棚卸資産と売上原価の会計処理 |
| Worksheet and Closing Entries | 精算表と締切仕訳 |
| Financial Statements | 財務諸表 |
| Basic Assumptions and GAAP | 基本的な前提と GAAP |
| Financial Statement Analysis | 財務諸表分析 |
| Internal Control | 内部統制 |
| Cash Control | 現金管理 |

## 2. Accounting Manager & Controller Level（配点 600 点）

| | |
|---|---|
| International Financial Reporting Standards and its Conceptual Framework | IFRS とその概念フレームワーク |
| Financial Statements | 財務諸表 |
| Fair Value Measurement | 公正価値測定 |
| Cash and Trade Receivables | 現金と売上債権 |
| Inventories | 棚卸資産 |
| Property, Plant and Equipment | 有形固定資産 |
| Intangible Assets | 無形資産 |
| Impairment of Property, Plant and Equipment and Intangible Assets | 有形固定資産および無形資産の減損 |
| Lease | リース |
| Financial Assets | 金融資産 |
| Financial Liabilities | 金融負債 |
| Provisions, Contingent Liabilities and Contingent Assets | 引当金、偶発負債および偶発資産 |
| Equity | 資本 |
| Revenue Recognition | 収益認識 |
| Employee Benefits | 従業員給付 |
| Income Taxes | 法人所得税 |
| Statement of Cash Flows | キャッシュ・フロー計算書 |
| Business Combinations / Consolidated Statements | 企業結合と連結 |
| The Effects of Changes in Foreign Exchange Rates | 為替レート変動の影響 |
| Accounting Policies, Changes in Accounting Estimates and Errors | 会計方針、会計上の見積りの変更および誤謬 |
| Earnings per Share | 1 株当たり利益 |
| Interim Financial Reporting | 期中財務報告 |
| Operating Segments | 事業セグメント |

# CONTENTS 〈目次〉

検定試験のご案内 ……………………………………………………………… ii

**問題編**

難易度
レベル

| Chapter 1 | International Financial Reporting Standards and its Conceptual Framework … | 1 ★★ |
| Chapter 2 | Financial Statements ……………………………… | 3 ★★ |
| Chapter 3 | Fair Value Measurement ……………………… | 7 ★★ |
| Chapter 4 | Cash and Trade Receivables …………………… | 9 ★ |
| Chapter 5 | Inventories ……………………………………… | 13 ★ |
| Chapter 6 | Property, Plant and Equipment ……………… | 19 ★ |
| Chapter 7 | Intangible Assets ……………………………… | 27 ★ |
| Chapter 8 | Impairment of Property, Plant and Equipment and Intangible Assets … | 31 ★ |
| Chapter 9 | Lease ……………………………………………… | 39 ★★ |
| Chapter 10 | Financial Assets ……………………………… | 45 ★★★ |
| Chapter 11 | Financial Liabilities ………………………… | 51 ★★ |
| Chapter 12 | Provisions, Contingent Liabilities and Contingent Assets… | 55 ★ |
| Chapter 13 | Equity …………………………………………… | 59 ★★ |
| Chapter 14 | Revenue Recognition ………………………… | 63 ★★★ |
| Chapter 15 | Employee Benefits …………………………… | 69 ★★★ |
| Chapter 16 | Income Taxes ………………………………… | 75 ★★★ |
| Chapter 17 | Statement of Cash Flows …………………… | 81 ★★ |
| Chapter 18 | Business Combinations / Consolidated Statements …… | 87 ★★★ |
| Chapter 19 | The Effects of Changes in Foreign Exchange Rates …… | 97 ★★★ |
| Chapter 20 | Accounting Policies, Changes in Accounting Estimates and Errors …101 ★ |
| Chapter 21 | Earnings per Share …………………………… | 105 ★★★ |
| Chapter 22 | Interim Financial Reporting ………………… | 109 ★★ |
| Chapter 23 | Operating Segments ………………………… | 111 ★★ |
| Appendix | Time Value of Money ………………………… | 115 |

# Contents

## 解答編

| | | |
|---|---|---|
| Chapter 1 | International Financial Reporting Standards and its Conceptual Framework | 119 |
| Chapter 2 | Financial Statements | 121 |
| Chapter 3 | Fair Value Measurement | 125 |
| Chapter 4 | Cash and Trade Receivables | 129 |
| Chapter 5 | Inventories | 133 |
| Chapter 6 | Property, Plant and Equipment | 139 |
| Chapter 7 | Intangible Assets | 149 |
| Chapter 8 | Impairment of Property, Plant and Equipment and Intangible Assets | 155 |
| Chapter 9 | Lease | 165 |
| Chapter 10 | Financial Assets | 171 |
| Chapter 11 | Financial Liabilities | 177 |
| Chapter 12 | Provisions, Contingent Liabilities and Contingent Assets | 183 |
| Chapter 13 | Equity | 187 |
| Chapter 14 | Revenue Recognition | 193 |
| Chapter 15 | Employee Benefits | 201 |
| Chapter 16 | Income Taxes | 209 |
| Chapter 17 | Statement of Cash Flows | 217 |
| Chapter 18 | Business Combinations / Consolidated Statements | 225 |
| Chapter 19 | The Effects of Changes in Foreign Exchange Rates | 237 |
| Chapter 20 | Accounting Policies, Changes in Accounting Estimates and Errors | 243 |
| Chapter 21 | Earnings per Share | 249 |
| Chapter 22 | Interim Financial Reporting | 253 |
| Chapter 23 | Operating Segments | 257 |
| Appendix | Time Value of Money | 261 |
| 過去問題 | 第37回 試験問題 | 265 |

# CHAPTER 1

# International Financial Reporting Standards and its Conceptual Framework

## International Financial Reporting Standards and its Conceptual Framework

### 1-1

Which of the following is included in the primary users to whom general purpose financial reports are directed?

(1) Consumers
(2) Investors
(3) Management
(4) Regulators
(5) All of the above

### 1-2

Which of the following is correct as one of the fundamental qualitative characteristics of useful financial information?

(1) Comparability
(2) Relevance
(3) Timeliness
(4) Understandability
(5) Verifiability

# CHAPTER 2

難易度レベル ★★☆

# Financial Statements

## Financial Statements

### 2-1

West Company recorded profit from continuing operations of $35,000 for the year ended 31 December 20X0. In addition, it declared and paid cash dividends of $9,000 and incurred an actuarial gain for 20X0 on remeasurements of defined benefit plans of $2,000 (net of tax). Compute West Company's profit and comprehensive income for 20X0.

| | Profit | Comprehensive income |
|---|---|---|
| (1) | $26,000 | $26,000 |
| (2) | $26,000 | $28,000 |
| (3) | $35,000 | $26,000 |
| (4) | $35,000 | $37,000 |
| (5) | $37,000 | $28,000 |

### 2-2

Which of the following is presented as a component of other comprehensive income in its financial statements?

a. Gain on revaluation of property, plant and equipment
b. Share of profit of associates
c. Exchange differences on translating foreign operations

(1) a. only
(2) b. only
(3) c. only
(4) a. and b. only
(5) a. and c. only

**2-3**

On 1 January 20X5, Moyes Ltd disposed of its foreign operation at a gain of £37,000. The exchange differences on translating the foreign operation are recognised in other comprehensive income and accumulated in equity. The credit balance of the exchange differences on translating the foreign operation in equity was £25,000 on 1 January 20X5.

In addition, Moyes Ltd acquired £200,000 of land for its own use on 1 January 20X5. It uses revaluation model for the land. The fair value of the land was £208,000 on 31 December 20X5.

These were only components of other comprehensive income for the year ended 31 December 20X5. What amount of other comprehensive income should Moyes Ltd report for the year ended 31 December 20X5?

(1) £(33,000)
(2) £(17,000)
(3) £( 4,000)
(4) £ 20,000
(5) £ 33,000

# CHAPTER 3

難易度レベル ★★☆

問題編

## Fair Value Measurement

## Fair Value Measurement

### 3-1

Regarding fair value measurements, which of the following is correct?

(1) Fair value is based on the entity-specific measurement.

(2) The market approach uses prices generated by forced transactions involving identical assets or liabilities.

(3) The income approach involves converting past cash flows into a single future value.

(4) The cost approach is based on the amount that currently would be required to replace the service capacity of an asset.

(5) All of the above

### 3-2

The following are statements regarding the fair value measurement.

a. It is most preferable to use quoted prices in active markets for identical assets or liabilities as inputs if such prices exist.

b. Level 2 inputs are observable inputs other than quoted prices in active markets for identical assets or liabilities.

c. Regardless of existences of observable inputs, a company can use level 3 inputs.

Select the most appropriate combination to indicate whether True or False.

|     | a.    | b.    | c.    |
|-----|-------|-------|-------|
| (1) | True  | True  | True  |
| (2) | True  | True  | False |
| (3) | True  | False | True  |
| (4) | False | True  | False |
| (5) | False | False | False |

8

問題編

# CHAPTER 4

難易度レベル ★☆☆

# Cash and
# Trade Receivables

Bookkeeping & Accounting Test for International Communication

# BATIC
Bookkeeper & Accountant Level

## Cash and Trade Receivables

**4-1**

Adam Company had the following account balances at 31 March 20X2:

| | |
|---|---:|
| Cash on hand | $ 200,000 |
| Demand deposits | 1,300,000 |
| Time deposit made on 31 March 20X2, with original maturity of six months from the date of opening the account | 500,000 |
| Bank overdrafts which are repayable on demand and an integral part of Adam's cash manegement | 14,000 |

At 31 March 20X2, the total amount of Adam's cash and cash equivalents is

(1) $1,486,000
(2) $1,500,000
(3) $1,514,000
(4) $1,986,000
(5) $2,000,000

## Cash and Trade Receivables

### 4-2

The following information relates to Hanson Corporation's accounts receivable for 20X0:

| | |
|---|---:|
| Accounts receivable on 1/1/ 20X0 | € 90,000 |
| Sales on credit for 20X0 | 780,000 |
| Sales returns for 20X0 | 22,000 |
| Accounts written off during 20X0 | 11,500 |
| Collections from customers during 20X0 | 630,000 |
| Allowance for doubtful accounts on 31/12/20X0 | 32,000 |

At 31 December 20X0, the correct balance of Hanson's accounts receivable is

(1)  € 206,500
(2)  € 174,500
(3)  € 150,000
(4)  €  58,000
(5)  None of the above

# Cash and Trade Receivables

## 4-3

Presented below is a provision matrix of Jessie Company's accounts receivable at 31 December 20X0:

| Days past due | Gross carrying amount | Default rate |
|---|---|---|
| Current | $180,000 | 1% |
| 1-30 days | 120,000 | 3% |
| 31-60 days | 90,000 | 6% |
| Over 60 days | 15,000 | 25% |

What is the appropriate balance for the allowance for doubtful accounts on 31 December 20X0?

(1) $ 9,500
(2) $12,000
(3) $14,550
(4) $18,000
(5) None of the above

問題編

# CHAPTER 5

難易度レベル ★ ☆ ☆

# Inventories

Bookkeeping & Accounting Test for International Communication

# BATIC
Bookkeeper & Accountant Level

## 5-1

Paddy Corporation purchased merchandise on 1 February 20X4. The following information shows the details of the costs incurred on Paddy, relating to its purchase of the merchandise:

| | |
|---|---:|
| Purchase price | £500,000 |
| Transportation costs | 18,000 |
| Trade discount | 400 |
| Interest on loans borrowed from a bank to | |
|    purchase the goods | 250 |

The interest on loans borrowed from a bank was directly attributable to the acquisition of the merchandise which is a qualifying asset. Assume that Paddy did not have any merchandise inventory before 1 February 20X4. What amount should be incurred in Paddy's inventory after Paddy recorded this transaction on its accounting book?

(1) £500,000
(2) £517,600
(3) £517,850
(4) £525,150
(5) None of the above

# Inventories

## 5-2

The following is taken from a record of Texas Corporation's transactions for the month of March 20X0:

| Date | Transaction | Unit | Unit Cost | Total Cost | Unit on hand |
|------|-------------|------|-----------|------------|--------------|
| 1/3/20X0 | Balance | 400 | $2 | $ 800 | 400 |
| 7/3/20X0 | Purchase | 400 | 4 | 1,600 | 800 |
| 17/3/20X0 | Sale | 600 | | | 200 |
| 22/3/20X0 | Purchase | 800 | 5 | 4,000 | 1,000 |
| 26/3/20X0 | Sale | 300 | | | 700 |

Texas uses the perpetual inventory method. Under the moving-average method, what amount should Texas report as inventory at 31 March 20X0?

(1) $2,100

(2) $3,220

(3) $4,550

(4) $5,000

(5) None of the above

# Inventories

## 5-3

The following information relates to the inventory at a fiscal year-end held by ABC Company.

|  | Item A | Item B | Item C |
|---|---|---|---|
| Quantity | 700 | 500 | 800 |
| Historical cost per unit | $ 80 | $ 95 | $ 60 |
| Replacement cost per unit | $ 70 | $ 90 | $ 55 |
| Estimated selling price per unit | $ 90 | $100 | $ 75 |
| Estimated cost to sell per unit | $ 15 | $ 20 | $ 10 |

What amount of inventory should ABC Company report in its financial statements at the fiscal year-end?

(1) $133,000

(2) $138,000

(3) $140,500

(4) $144,500

(5) $151,500

## 5-4

Which of the following is not correct regarding inventory valuation?

(1) LIFO is prohibited to evaluate inventory cost.

(2) The amount previously written down may be reversed, when there is clear evidence that net realisable value increases.

(3) Inventories should be written down to net realisable value, when the cost of inventories are not recoverable.

(4) The recoverability of the cost of inventories is tested to compare the cost of inventory item with the fair value of the item.

(5) The specific identification method is appropriate for items which are not ordinary interchangeable and segregated for specific projects.

問題編

# CHAPTER 6

難易度レベル ★ ☆ ☆

# Property, Plant and Equipment

Bookkeeping & Accounting Test for International Communication

# BATIC

Bookkeeper & Accountant Level

# Property, Plant and Equipment

## 6-1

Due to the needs of its business operation, Jackson Company purchased machine at a cost of $72,000 on 1 January 20X4. The following are expenditures relating to the machine during 20X4.

| | |
|---|---:|
| Freight on purchase | $3,600 |
| Costs of bringing and installing the machine to the place of intended operation | 2,900 |
| Costs of testing whether the machine is functioning properly while bringing it to the condition to be capable of intended operation | 4,400 |
| Costs of testing after the machine is functioning properly after bringing it to the condition to be capable of intended operation | 2,700 |
| Maintenance costs of day-to-day servicing of the machine | 1,500 |

On Jackson's accounting book, what amount should be recorded as the cost of the machine?

(1) $75,600
(2) $82,900
(3) $84,400
(4) $85,600
(5) $87,100

Property, Plant and Equipment

## Questions 2 and 3 are based on the following:

On 1 January 20X5, Ferguson Plc started constructing its own factory and borrowed £200,000 with 5% interest from a bank for the construction. It estimated that the construction period will be about 16 months. In addition to the above borrowing for the construction, Ferguson had the following debts during 20X5.

| | |
|---|---:|
| 8%, 5-years bonds issued 1 January 20X3, | |
| with interest payable annually | £180,000 |
| 6%, 3-years note dated 1 January 20X4, | |
| with interest payable annually | 120,000 |

Ferguson made the following payments for the construction during 20X5:

1 January  £200,000
1 October    100,000

# Property, Plant and Equipment

## 6-2

Ferguson Company uses the weighted-average accumulated expenditures as a reasonable approximation of the expenditures to which the capitalisation rate is applied. Calculate the amount of expenditures on the factory during 20X5.

(1) £100,000

(2) £200,000

(3) £225,000

(4) £300,000

(5) None of the above

## 6-3

Compute the interest cost to be capitalised during 20X5.

(1) £10,000

(2) £11,250

(3) £11,800

(4) £26,200

(5) £31,600

# Property, Plant and Equipment

## 6-4

Spalletti Company has a truck which was purchased at a cost of €60,000. On 31 December 20X3, it replaced tyres of the truck to new tyres costing €8,000. It paid €7,000 for new tyres after exchanging the old tyres.

Regarding the truck, Spalletti keeps accounting records based on the significant components and depreciates them separately. The following information relates to the significant parts of the truck on 31 December 20X3.

|                          | Acquisition cost | Accumulated depreciation |
|--------------------------|:----------------:|:------------------------:|
| Engine and transmission  | €15,000          | € 7,800                  |
| Structure                | 36,000           | 12,000                   |
| Tyres                    | 9,000            | 6,000                    |

What amount of gain or loss should Spalletti record on the replacement of the tyres?

## Property, Plant and Equipment

### 6-5

XYZ Company owns a land for its business. At the beginning of an accounting period, the carrying amount of the land was $750,000 and there was a credit balance of the revaluation surplus for the land, $12,000. At the end of the same accounting period, the fair value for the land was determined $730,000 by an appraisal. XYZ Company uses the revaluation model for the land. What amount of the loss should XYZ record in other comprehensive income as a result of a revaluation for the land?

(1) $0
(2) $ 8,000
(3) $12,000
(4) $20,000
(5) $32,000

### 6-6

ABC Company sold its old equipment to XYZ Company for $100,000 on 1 November 20X0. The equipment was originally purchased at the cost of $150,000, with residual value of $15,000. The accumulated depreciation as at 1 November 20X0 was $54,000. What amount should ABC recognise as gain (loss) on the sale?

(1) $( 19,000)
(2) $ 0
(3) $  4,000
(4) $ 11,000
(5) $ 100,000

Property, Plant and Equipment

## Questions 7 and 8 are based on the following:

Omiya Flowers owns two buildings. Management has decided to sell these buildings and expects to change the classification of these buildings from assets held for use to assets held for sale.

| 6-7 |

Which of the following would prevent Omiya from changing the classification?

(1)  Two buildings are readily available for sale in their present condition.

(2)  Omiya started to advertise the sale in real estate magazines.

(3)  Omiya expects to complete the sales of buildings in ten months.

(4)  Omiya may withdraw the plan if the buildings have not been sold in ten months.

(5)  None of the above

## Property, Plant and Equipment

### 6-8

Assume that the two buildings to be sold were classified as assets held for sale on 1 July 20X7.

| | Acquisition date | Cost | Residual value | Depreciation period | Fair value less costs to sell as at 1/7/20X7 | Depreciation method |
|---|---|---|---|---|---|---|
| Building A | 1/1/20X0 | ¥1,000,000 | ¥ 10,000 | 9 years | ¥400,000 | Straight-line |
| Building B | 1/7/20X2 | ¥1,200,000 | ¥100,000 | 10 years | ¥490,000 | Straight-line |

Based on this situation, prepare the required journal entry relating to the classification.

Ignore the journal entries to change the classification of the buildings.

(1) No journal entries

(2) Dr Depreciation Expense 110,000
     Cr Accumulated Depreciation 110,000
     Dr Impairment Loss 160,000
     Cr Fixed Asset 160,000

(3) Dr Depreciation Expense 220,000
     Cr Accumulated Depreciation 220,000
     Dr Impairment Loss 105,000
     Cr Fixed Asset 105,000

(4) Dr Impairment Loss 215,000
     Cr Fixed Asset 215,000

(5) Dr Depreciation Expense 220,000
     Cr Accumulated Depreciation 220,000

問題編

# CHAPTER 7

難易度レベル

# Intangible Assets

Bookkeeping & Accounting Test for International Communication

## BATIC
Bookkeeper & Accountant Level

## Intangible Assets

### 7-1

Select most appropriate combination to fill in the following blanks.

When an entity recognises an item as an intangible asset, the item is required to be [　　　A　　　] by the entity as a result of past event and [　　　B　　　] to distinguish it from goodwill, and furthermore, it is required that [　　　C　　　] are expected to flow into the entity from it.

|  | A | B | C |
|---|---|---|---|
| (1) | Certified | Alternative | Cash and cash equivalents |
| (2) | Certified | Identifiable | Future economic benefits |
| (3) | Controlled | Alternative | Cash and cash equivalents |
| (4) | Controlled | Identifiable | Future economic benefits |
| (5) | Controlled | Identifiable | Cash and cash equivalents |

# Intangible Assets

## 7-2

Rosario Ltd is developing a new product. Expenditure for the product was incurred € 250,000 between 1 January 20X5 and 31 August 20X5, and €17,000 between 1 September 20X5 and 31 December 20X5. It can demonstrate that the new product met the criteria for recognition as an intangible asset at 1 September 20X5. What amount should Rosario Ltd recognise as an expense and an asset in its financial statements for 20X5?

|     | Expense   | Asset     |
|-----|-----------|-----------|
| (1) | €0        | €0        |
| (2) | €250,000  | €0        |
| (3) | €267,000  | €0        |
| (4) | €250,000  | € 17,000  |
| (5) | € 0       | €267,000  |

# Intangible Assets

## 7-3

On 1 January 20X0, Smith Plc bought a copyright for a best selling novel for £500,000. In addition, Smith paid £20,000 in legal fees to register the copyright during 20X0. Its remaining contractual right was 50 years. The pattern in which the copyright's future economic benefits are expected to be consumed cannot be determined reliably. There is no commitment by a third party to purchase it and the active market for it does not exist. Smith Plc uses the cost model to account for the copyright.

How much amortisation expense regarding the copyright should Smith report in its income statement for the year ended 31 December 20X0?

(1) £10,000
(2) £10,400
(3) £12,500
(4) £13,000
(5) None of the above

## 7-4

On 1 January 20X0, Park Company acquired Shell Company in a business combination recognising goodwill of € 50,000. At 31 December 20X0, annual related impairment test of goodwill showed no impairment.

Compute the amortisation expense for the goodwill during 20X0.

# CHAPTER 8

問題編

難易度レベル ★ ☆ ☆

# Impairment of Property, Plant and Equipment and Intangible Assets

Bookkeeping & Accounting Test for International Communication

**BATIC**

Bookkeeper & Accountant Level

Impairment of Property, Plant and Equipment and Intangible Assets

## 8-1

Which of the following is not correct regarding accounting for impairment?

(1) The recoverable amount is the greater of an asset's fair value less selling cost and its value in use.

(2) When it is impossible to determine the recoverable amount for an individual asset, the recoverable amount of the cash-generating unit to which the asset belongs should be estimated.

(3) It is not allowed to reverse an impairment loss previously recognised.

(4) Under the cost model, an impairment loss is recognised in profit or loss.

(5) If the carrying amount of an asset exceeds its recoverable amount, the amount of the excess is recognised as an impairment loss.

# Impairment of Property, Plant and Equipment and Intangible Assets

## 8-2

Miyazaki Company bought machinery for its business in the amount of $60,000 on 1 January 20X2. Depreciation of the machinery is computed by using the straight-line method over its estimated useful life of 5 years with no residual value. On 31 December 20X2, an impairment test was performed and showed that the present value of expected future cash flows from the use of the machinery was only $30,000. The fair value less cost of disposal of the machinery on 31 December 20X2 was $25,000. What amount should Miyazaki Company recognise as impairment loss for the year ended 31 December 20X2?

(1) $12,000
(2) $18,000
(3) $20,000
(4) $30,000
(5) $40,000

Chapter 8

Impairment of Property, Plant and Equipment and Intangible Assets

## Questions 3 and 4 are based on the following:

On 31 December 20X4, Valdez Company performed an impairment test for equipment as there was an indication of impairment. The remaining useful life of the equipment was two years as at 31 December 20X4.The following data relate to the possible cash flows from the use and disposal of the equipment in each remaining year.

| Year | Possible cash flow | Probability |
|------|-------------------|-------------|
| 20X5 | €40,000 | 20% |
|      | 80,000 | 50% |
|      | 90,000 | 30% |
| 20X6 | €20,000 | 30% |
|      | 40,000 | 60% |
|      | 60,000 | 10% |

Valdez Company uses the expected cash flow approach to estimate future cash flows of the equipment and determined that the appropriate discount rate for this estimation was 7%.

Impairment of Property, Plant and Equipment and Intangible Assets

## 8-3

Calculate the future cash flow of the equipment in 20X5.

(1) €40,000

(2) €70,000

(3) €75,000

(4) €80,000

(5) €90,000

## 8-4

Calculate the value in use of the equipment. If necessary, round to the nearest euro.

(1) € 96,952

(2) €101,537

(3) €104,813

(4) €111,000

(5) €120,000

## 8-5

On 1 January 20X4, Spartan Company purchased equipment for ¥5,000,000, with a five-year life and no residual value. It is measured using the cost model and depreciated using the straight-line method. On 31 December 20X5, due to the deterioration of its business environment, Spartan recognised an impairment loss of ¥600,000 for the equipment. On 31 December 20X6, the business environment improved and Spartan determined that recoverable amount of the equipment was ¥1,700,000. Which of the following journal entries should Spartan make for the equipment after depreciation on 31 December 20X6?

(1) Dr Accumulated depreciation and
     impairment losses                                    1,100,000
       Cr Other comprehensive income                                   1,100,000

(2) Dr Accumulated depreciation and
     impairment losses                                      100,000
       Cr Reversal of impairment loss                                    100,000

(3) Dr Accumulated depreciation and
     impairment losses                                      600,000
       Cr Reversal of impairment loss                                    600,000

(4) Dr Other comprehensive income                           300,000
       Cr Revaluation surplus                                            300,000

(5) No journal entry is necessary.

## Impairment of Property, Plant and Equipment and Intangible Assets

### 8-6

Ferguson Ltd has three cash-generating units, Unit X, Unit Y and Unit Z. On 31 December 20X6, as there was an adverse change in the market environment in which Ferguson operates, it performed impairment tests of each of its cash-generating units. The carrying amounts of X, Y and Z are €120,000, €180,000 and €300,000 respectively. These amounts do not include goodwill.

The assets of each cash-generating unit are as follows:

|       | Unit X   | Unit Y    | Unit Z    |
|-------|----------|-----------|-----------|
| Plant | €70,000  | €112,500  | €187,500  |
| Land  | 50,000   | 67,500    | 112,500   |

The recoverable amounts of each cash-generating unit are as follows:

| Unit X | €160,000 |
|--------|----------|
| Unit Y | 210,000  |
| Unit Z | 340,000  |

Ferguson also has two corporate assets, a head office and a research centre. The carrying amounts of the head office and the research centre are €150,000 and €90,000 respectively. The relative carrying amounts of the cash-generating units are a reasonable indication of the proportion of the head office devoted to each cash-generating unit. The carrying amount of research centre cannot be allocated on a reasonable basis to the three units.

Calculate the carrying amount of each corporate asset after allocating the impairment loss. If necessary, round the amount to the nearest euro.

# CHAPTER 9

問題編

難易度レベル

## Lease

Bookkeeping & Accounting Test for International Communication

# BATIC
Bookkeeper & Accountant Level

Lease

## Questions 1 through 3 are based on the following:

West Corporation (Lessee) entered into a lease contract with Arban Incorporated (Lessor) for new equipment.
Information is as follows:

| | |
|---|---:|
| Commencement of lease term | 31 December 20X1 |
| Lease term | 5 years |
| Annual lease payment payable at end of each year | $2,500 |
| Estimated useful life of equipment | 9 years |
| West's incremental borrowing rate | 12% |
| Implicit interest rate in lease known to West | 10% |
| Present value of an ordinary annuity of 1 for 5 periods at 10% | 3.791 |
| 12% | 3.605 |

The lease contract does not contain a renewal option and the title of the leased equipment is transferred to West from Arban at the termination of the lease. The carrying amount of the leased equipment in Arban's records was $6,500.

### 9-1

What amount of lease liability should West recognise in its statement of financial position as at 31 December 20X1? Amount should be rounded to the nearest dollar, if necessary.

Lease

## 9-2

What amount of depreciation expense should be recorded in West's 20X2 income statement? West has adopted the straight-line method with no residual value for depreciation. Amount should be rounded to the nearest dollar, if necessary.

## 9-3

Fill in the blanks of journal entries below for Arban at the beginning of the lease.

Dr  Lease receivable      [          ]
      Cr Sales                         [          ]

Dr  Cost of sales         [          ]
      Cr Inventory                     [          ]

# Lease

## Questions 4 through 6 are based on the following:

XYZ Company leased new equipment from a leasing company. The terms of the lease do not contain a bargain purchase option or transfer of the title at the end of the lease. The additional information relating to the lease is as follows:

| | |
|---|---|
| Commencement of lease term | 1 January 20X0 |
| Lease term | 8 years |
| Annual lease payment payable at end of each year | $1,200 |
| Fair value of equipment | $6,402 |
| Estimated useful life of equipment | 10 years |
| XYZ's incremental borrowing rate | 11% |
| Lessor's implicit interest rate known to XYZ | 10% |
| | |
| Depreciation | straight-line  (no residual value) |
| | |
| Present value of an ordinary annuity of 1 for 8 periods at 10% | 5.335 |
| 11% | 5.146 |

The amount should be rounded off to the nearest dollar.

Lease

## 9-4

What amount of interest expense should XYZ recognise for the year ended 31 December 20X0?

(1) $  640
(2) $  679
(3) $  704
(4) $  960
(5) $1,200

## 9-5

What amount of lease liability should XYZ recognise as at 31 December 20X0?

(1) $5,654
(2) $5,842
(3) $6,175
(4) $6,402
(5) $8,400

Chapter 9

Lease

## 9-6

What amount of depreciation expense should XYZ recognise for the year ended 31 December 20X0?

(1) $0
(2) $618
(3) $640
(4) $771
(5) $800

# CHAPTER 10

難易度レベル ★★★

# Financial Assets

# Financial Assets

## 10-1

Jones Ltd purchased £100,000 equity securities on 1 March 20X5. Jones classified the securities as measured at fair value and elected to present in other comprehensive income subsequent changes in the fair value.

On 1 October 20X5, Jones received £4,000 as cash dividends. On 31 December 20X5, the fair value of the securities was £105,000.

What amount should Jones include in other comprehensive income for the year ended 31 December 20X5?

(1) £0
(2) £1,000
(3) £4,000
(4) £5,000
(5) £9,000

Financial Assets

## Questions 2 and 3 are based on the following:

On 1 January 20X5, Pineapple Inc. purchased equity instrument with $10,000 cash and designated it as measured at fair value through other comprehensive income.

Fair values of the instrument were as follows.

| | |
|---|---|
| On 31 December 20X5 | $ 9,000 |
| On 31 December 20X6 | 12,000 |

### 10-2

What amount of other comprehensive income should Pineapple Inc. recognise for the year ended 31 December 20X6?

(1) $0

(2) $2,000 on the debit side

(3) $2,000 on the credit side

(4) $3,000 on the debit side

(5) $3,000 on the credit side

Financial Assets

## 10-3

Pineapple Inc. sold the equity instrument on 1 January 20X7 for $13,000 cash. Which of the following journal entries should it make on 1 January 20X7?

| | | | |
|---|---|---|---|
| (1) Dr Cash | 13,000 | | |
| Cr Financial asset | | 10,000 | |
| Gain on sale of financial asset | | 3,000 | |
| (2) Dr Cash | 13,000 | | |
| Cr Financial asset | | 12,000 | |
| Gain on sale of financial asset | | 1,000 | |
| (3) Dr Cash | 13,000 | | |
| Cr Financial asset | | 10,000 | |
| OCI* | | 3,000 | |
| (4) Dr Cash | 13,000 | | |
| Cr Financial asset | | 12,000 | |
| OCI | | 1,000 | |
| (5) Dr Cash | 13,000 | | |
| OCI | 2,000 | | |
| Cr Financial asset | | 12,000 | |
| Gain on sale of financial asset | | 3,000 | |

*OCI = Other Comprehensive Income

# Financial Assets

## 10-4

On 31 December 20X5, Todd Corporation purchased € 5,000,000 debt securities which were classified as measured at fair value through other comprehensive income. At the purchase, Todd determined that the securities were not credit-impaired.

The following information relates to the expected credit loss on 31 December 20X5.

| | |
|---|---|
| 12-month expected credit loss | € 300,000 |
| Lifetime expected credit loss | € 500,000 |

Complete the following journal entries that Todd Corporation should make on 31 December 20X5.

Dr Financial asset—FVOCI          [            ]
   Impairment loss (profit or loss)     [            ]
      Cr Cash                                   [            ]
         Other comprehensive income       [            ]

## Financial Assets

### 10-5

Smith plc sold its accounts receivable of £40,000 to a factor without recourse. On the sale, Smith transferred the contractual rights to receive the cash flows of the accounts receivable. The factor charged 3% service fee. What amount should Smith record as loss on the sale of accounts receivable?

(1) £0

(2) £ 1,200

(3) £38,800

(4) £40,000

(5) None of the above

# CHAPTER 11

問題編

難易度レベル ★★☆

# Financial Liabilities

# Financial Liabilities

## 11-1

Pegasus Corporation issued $1,000,000 of its 10-year, 6% term bonds on 1 September 20X0. The bonds were dated 1 July 20X0 and sold to yield 8% with total proceeds of $864,000 plus accrued interest. Pegasus pays interest semiannually on 1 January and 1 July. Pegasus did not designate the bonds as measured at fair value through profit or loss. What amount should be reported as interest payable in Pegasus's 31 December 20X0 statement of financial position?

(1) $20,000
(2) $30,000
(3) $34,560
(4) $40,000
(5) None of the above

## 11-2

Stuart Corporation issued 8% bonds in the amount of € 500,000 on 1 January 20X1. The bonds mature on 1 January 20X9. The bonds were issued at par. Interest is payable semiannually on 1 July and 1 January. Stuart did not designate the bonds as measured at fair value through profit or loss. Prepare the journal entries to record each of the following transactions.

(a) The issuance of the bonds
(b) The payment of interest on 1 July 20X1
(c) The accrual of interest on 31 March 20X2

# Financial Liabilities

## 11-3

BBB Ltd issued the following straight bonds.

| | |
|---|---|
| Issue date | 1 January 20X1 |
| Mature date | 31 December 20X4 |
| Face amount | € 80,000 |
| Face rate | 4% |
| Yield rate | 5% |
| Payment of interest | Annually on 31 December |

BBB did not designate the bonds as measured at fair value through profit or loss.

For calculation, use the following present value information:

| | |
|---|---|
| Present value of an ordinary annuity of 1 for 4 years at 5% | 3.5459 |
| Present value of 1 for 4 years at 5% | 0.8227 |

Calculate the following amounts. Round each amount to the nearest euro, if necessary.

(1) Issue price
(2) Discount on bonds payable as at 1 January 20X1
(3) Interest expense for the year ended 31 December 20X1
(4) Discount on bonds payable as at 31 December 20X1

**CHAPTER 12**

問題編

難易度レベル

# Provisions, Contingent Liabilities and Contingent Assets

Bookkeeping & Accounting Test for International Communication

**BATIC**

Bookkeeper & Accountant Level

Provisions, Contingent Liabilities and Contingent Assets

## Questions 1 and 2 are based on the following:

The following situations relate to Nara Motors.

a. Nara brought a lawsuit against Kyoto Company for damages from Kyoto's unauthorised use of Nara's patent. Nara will probably win and get ¥70,000,000 from the defendant.

b. Residents filed a lawsuit against Nara for health damage caused by gaseous emissions from its plant. According to the lawyer, Nara would probably lose the lawsuit and pay between ¥100,000,000 and ¥300,000,000. The best estimate of the amount to pay was ¥250,000,000.

c. A consumer sued Nara for bodily injury caused by a defect in Nara's product. The lawyer commented that it was not probable that Nara would lose the lawsuit. However, he also commented that, if Nara lost the lawsuit, it would pay approximately ¥600,000,000.

d. A former employee claims that he is entitled to receive ¥100,000,000 reward for developing a patent. The lawyer judged that the company would not lose the lawsuit, since the crucial part of the patent was developed by other colleagues.

# Provisions, Contingent Liabilities and Contingent Assets

## 12-1

What amount should Nara recognise as provisions?

(1) ¥180,000,000

(2) ¥250,000,000

(3) ¥600,000,000

(4) ¥800,000,000

(5) ¥900,000,000

## 12-2

Which cases are not recognised as provisions but disclosed in the note?

(1) (a) and (b) only.

(2) (a) and (c) only.

(3) (a), (c) and (d) only.

(4) (b), (c) and (d) only.

(5) (c) and (d) only.

## Provisions, Contingent Liabilities and Contingent Assets

### 12-3

The board of Hung Company decided to withdraw from one of its businesses and expected the following costs would incur relating to the restructuring.

(a) A penalty cost to terminate a long-term lease on an asset used in the business
(b) Costs of moving some assets of the business to other businesses
(c) Costs of retraining employees who will be shifted to other businesses
(d) Future operating losses expected to incur by the completion of the withdrawal
(e) Investment in new software system as a result of the withdrawal
(f) Onerous contract provisions relating to the withdrawal

The restructuring plan met the recognition criteria for provision. Which of the above cost(s) should be included in the restructuring provision?

(1) (a) and (d) only
(2) (a) and (f) only
(3) (a), (b) and (e) only
(4) (a), (b) and (f) only
(5) (a), (c) and (e) only

# CHAPTER 13

問題編

難易度レベル ★★☆

Equity

Bookkeeping & Accounting Test for International Communication
BATIC
Bookkeeper & Accountant Level

# Equity

## 13-1

Dart Company had 50,000 ordinary shares outstanding at 1 April 20X0. Dart declared 2 for 1 share split on 15 June. At that time, the market value of the share was $70 per share. Dart declared a $1 per share cash dividend on 30 November. No other transaction occurred. As at 31 December 20X0, what amount should Dart report as dividends payable?

(1) $0
(2) $100,000
(3) $150,000
(4) $225,000
(5) None of the above

# Equity

## 13-2

On 1 July 20X0, Klee Company started its business and issued 40,000 of ordinary shares at $10 par share and credited share capital for the full amount. Klee repurchased 5,000 shares at $200,000 on 1 October 20X2, and sold 3,000 shares of treasury shares at $135,000 on 31 December 20X2.

Which of the following journal entries correctly records the retirement of treasury shares?

(1) Dr Cash          135,000

    Share Premium—treasury       135,000

(2) Dr Cash          135,000

    Cr Share capital         15,000

     Treasury shares        120,000

(3) Dr Cash          135,000

    Cr Treasury shares        135,000

(4) Dr Cash          135,000

    Cr Share premium—treasury      15,000

     Treasury shares        120,000

(5) No journal entry is necessary.

# Equity

## 13-3

On 31 December 20X0, ABC Company issued convertible bonds, maturing on 31 December 20X2, with total proceeds of $70,000. On that issue date, the fair value of the liability component of the bonds was $50,000, and the fair value of the equity component of the bonds was $24,000. How should ABC Company present the convertible bonds on its balance sheet as at 31 December 20X0?

|  | Liability | Equity |
|---|---|---|
| (1) | $0 | $70,000 |
| (2) | $50,000 | $0 |
| (3) | $50,000 | $20,000 |
| (4) | $50,000 | $24,000 |
| (5) | $70,000 | $0 |

**CHAPTER 14**

難易度レベル ★★★

問題編

# Revenue Recognition

Bookkeeping & Accounting Test for International Communication

**BATIC**
Bookkeeper & Accountant Level

# Revenue Recognition

## 14-1

Under IFRS 15, which of the following is most appropriate as one of the criteria which should be met when a company accounts for a contract with a customer?

(1) It is not expected that the contract has an effect on the amount of company's future cash flows.

(2) It is probable that the company will obtain control of the goods or services to be transferred as a result of the company's performance.

(3) The company approved the contract in writing without commitment to perform its obligations.

(4) The company can identify the rights of each party for the goods or services to be transferred.

(5) The company leaves open the payment terms for the goods or services to be transferred.

# Revenue Recognition

## 14-2

On 1 January 20X4, Venger Company made a 2-year contract with a customer to clean the customer's offices on a weekly basis. On the same date, it assessed that each of the weekly cleaning services is distinct. The weekly cleaning services are a series of distinct services which are substantially the same and have the same pattern of transfer to the customer. The customer promised to pay €48,000 per year which was the stand-alone selling price of the services as at 1 January 20X4.

On 31 December 20X4, the contract was modified and the service fee for 20X5 was reduced to €45,000. On the same date, the contract was extended for additional 2 years and the customer agreed to pay €42,000 at the beginning of each additional year. The remaining services to be provided are distinct. As at 1 January 20X5, the stand-alone selling price of the services was €45,000.

What amount should Venger Company recognise as revenue from this contract per year over the remaining 3 years?

(1) €42,000

(2) €43,000

(3) €45,000

(4) €46,500

(5) €48,000

# Revenue Recognition

## Questions 3 and 4 are based on the following:

On 1 January 20X0, Sky Construction Company made a long-term contract to construct a shopping centre complex for a customer on customer-owned land for promised consideration of $4,200,000. It accounts for the bundle of goods and services in the contract as a single performance obligation which is satisfied over time. It uses the input method based on costs incurred to measure its progress toward complete satisfaction of the performance obligation. The following data are available for the year ended 31 December 20X0.

| | |
|---|---|
| Contract costs incurred to date | $1,000,000 |
| Estimated total contract costs | 4,000,000 |
| Progress billings during the year | 1,500,000 |
| Cash collection | 1,100,000 |

### 14-3

What amount should Sky recognise as revenue for 20X0?

(1) $1,050,000
(2) $1,100,000
(3) $1,400,000
(4) $1,500,000
(5) $3,200,000

## Revenue Recognition

### 14-4

What amount should Sky recognise as gross profit for 20X0?

(1) $ 50,000
(2) $100,000
(3) $200,000
(4) $400,000
(5) $500,000

### 14-5

Muller Company entered into a contract to operate a Bale Plc's data centre for 6 years. To obtain the contract, it incurred €12,000 of selling commission costs and expected to recover those costs through future fees for the services. Before performing the services, it built a technology platform that interfaces with Bale's system. The following costs incurred to build the technology platform.

| | |
|---|---|
| Hardware | €150,000 |
| Software | 100,000 |
| Migration and testing of data centre | 80,000 |

The above costs related to activities to fulfil the contract but did not transfer goods or services to Bale Plc. Muller Company estimated that the cost of migration and testing would not be recoverable.

What amount of the incremental costs to obtain the contract and the costs to fulfil the contract should Muller Company recognise as assets in accordance with IFRS 15?

|  | Incremental costs to obtain the contract | Costs to fulfil the contract |
|-----|------------|------------|
| (1) | € 0 | € 0 |
| (2) | € 0 | € 80,000 |
| (3) | € 12,000 | € 0 |
| (4) | € 12,000 | € 100,000 |
| (5) | € 12,000 | € 250,000 |

## 14-6

City Ltd sent £40,000 of merchandise on consignment to Cosmos Company. Cosmos Company sold half of the merchandise for £36,000 and notified City Ltd of the sales. The commission of Cosmos Company was 20% of the sales price to its customers. City Ltd is a principal and control the merchandise before which is transferred to the customers. Cosmos Company is an agent and sells the merchandise on behalf of City Ltd.

What amount should Cosmos Company recognise as revenue for this sale?

(1) £ 7,200
(2) £ 8,000
(3) £18,000
(4) £20,000
(5) £36,000

**CHAPTER 15**

# Employee Benefits

## Employee Benefits

### 15-1

The following relates to a company's defined benefit pension plan. The company's fiscal year ends on 31 December.

| | |
|---|---:|
| Present value of the defined benefit obligation as at 31 December 20X6 | €56,000 |
| Fair value of plan assets as at 31 December 20X6 | 62,000 |
| Asset ceiling as at 31 December 20X6 | 4,000 |

Determine the amount of net defined benefit liability or asset as at 31 December 20X6.

# Employee Benefits

## Questions 2 through 5 are based on the following:

The following information relates to ABC Company's defined benefit pension plan. Ignore income taxes.

| | |
|---|---:|
| **On 1 January 20X8:** | |
| Present value of defined benefit obligation | |
| including past service cost | $2,500,000 |
| Fair value of plan assets | 2,340,000 |
| Past service cost* | 620,000 |
| | |
| **During 20X8:** | |
| Current service cost | $630,000 |
| Return on plan asset | 190,000 |
| Contributions | 50,000 |
| Benefit paid | 30,000 |
| | |
| **On 31 December 20X8:** | |
| Present value of defined benefit obligation | |
| including actuarial loss | $3,410,000 |
| Fair value of plan assets | 2,550,000 |
| Actuarial loss** | 210,000 |
| | |
| Discount rate: 4% | |

\* The past service cost arose, because the pension plan was amended on 1 January 20X8.

\*\* The actuarial loss arose, because some assumptions related to future employee turnover were amended at the end of 20X8.

There was no effect of the asset ceiling on 31 December 20X7.

## Employee Benefits

### 15-2

As at 31 December 20X8, net defined benefit liability or asset is:

(1) $3,410,000 of liability

(2) $1,370,000 of liability

(3) $   860,000 of liability

(4) $   210,000 of asset

(5) $2,550,000 of asset

### 15-3

For the year ended 31 December 20X8, the amount of net interest is:

(1) $     6,400

(2) $   93,600

(3) $100,000

(4) $102,000

(5) $193,600

### 15-4

For the year ended 31 December 20X8, the amount of defined benefit cost in profit or loss is:

(1) $   636,400

(2) $   820,000

(3) $1,250,000

(4) $1,256,400

(5) $1,440,000

# Employee Benefits

## 15-5

For the year ended 31 December 20X8, the amount of defined benefit cost in other comprehensive income is:

(1) $ 20,000
(2) $113,600
(3) $210,000
(4) $306,400
(5) $400,000

## 15-6

On 1 January 20X5, Black Company granted employees share options to purchase 10,000 shares of Black's ordinary share at $25 per share when the market price of the share was $25 and the fair value of each share option was $6. The option will be exercisable on 1 January 20X8, after the employees fulfil the required services. On 31 December 20X5, the market price of the share and the fair value of the share option were $23 and $2.5 respectively.

What amount of compensation expense should Black recognise for 20X5?

(1) $0
(2) $ 20,000
(3) $ 25,000
(4) $ 60,000
(5) $140,000

# Employee Benefits

## 15-7

Employees of a company were granted the following share options on 1 January 20X5:

|         | Number of share options | Fair value of share option |
|---------|-------------------------|----------------------------|
| Plan A  | 1,000                   | $10                        |
| Plan B  | 1,000                   | $12                        |

Share options in Plan A are exercisable on 1 January 20X6. These options were given as reward for employees' performance in 20X4.

Share options in Plan B are exercisable on 1 January 20X8 after employees complete required services.

What amount should the company recognise as compensation expense for 20X5?

(1) $0

(2) $ 4,000

(3) $10,000

(4) $14,000

(5) $22,000

CHAPTER 16

問題編

難易度レベル

# Income Taxes

Bookkeeping & Accounting Test for International Communication

BATIC

Bookkeeper & Accountant Level

# Income Taxes

## Questions 1 and 2 are based on the following:

AAA Company started business at 1 January 20X0 and had revenues of $200,000 for accounting purpose and $170,000 for tax purpose in 20X0. The difference was temporary. AAA also had expenses of $100,000 for both accounting and tax purpose. AAA has a 30% tax rate.

### 16-1

What is AAA's income tax payable for 20X0?

(1) $ 9,000
(2) $21,000
(3) $30,000
(4) $51,000
(5) None of the above

### 16-2

What amount of deferred tax liability should AAA report in its 20X0 statement of financial position?

(1) $ 9,000
(2) $21,000
(3) $30,000
(4) $39,000
(5) None of the above

Income Taxes

## 16-3

Fulham plc reported £77,000 of warranty expense included in accounting profit for the year ended 31December 20X3. £20,000 of the warranty expense were deductible in 20X3 and the rest was expected to be deductible in 20X4 for tax reporting purposes. The enacted tax rate is 30% for 20X3 and thereafter.

What amount should Fulham report as current or non-current deferred tax asset in its statement of financial position as at 31 December 20X3?

|     | Current  | Non-current |
|-----|----------|-------------|
| (1) | —        | £  6,000    |
| (2) | —        | £17,100     |
| (3) | —        | £23,100     |
| (4) | £  6,000 | £17,100     |
| (5) | £17,100  | —           |

# Income Taxes

## Questions 4 through 6 are based on the following:

Apricot Company, a U.S. company, was founded on 1 January 20X0 and reported $39,000 of profit before tax for 20X0. The following information relates to income tax for 20X0.

- Profit before tax included interest income from municipal bonds, $2,300, and a fine payment, $1,000, both of which were permanently non-taxable and non-deductible for tax purposes, respectively.
- Profit before tax also included warranty expense of $4,400, of which only $1,000 was deductible for tax purposes in 20X0.
- Apricot Company uses different depreciation methods for tax and financial reporting. The table below indicates the tax basis and the book basis of depreciable assets at the end of each year.

|            | 20X0      | 20X1      | 20X2     | 20X3  |
|------------|-----------|-----------|----------|-------|
| Tax basis  | $15,000   | $ 7,000   | $2,000   | $0    |
| Book basis | 20,000    | 10,000    | 0        | 0     |

- The enacted tax rate is 30% for 20X0 and thereafter.

Offset deferred tax assets and liabilities and assume that deferred tax assets are fully recoverable, if any.

### 16-4

Calculate the amount to be reported as income tax payable in the statement of financial position as at 31 December 20X0.

## Income Taxes

### 16-5

Make the journal entry to record income tax expense—deferred for 20X0 financial statements.

Dr

   Cr

### 16-6

Calculate the amount to be reported as profit for the year in the statement of profit or loss for the year ended 31 December 20X0.

# Income Taxes

## 16-7

Onecent Ltd. made the following journal entry to record deferred tax asset due to $60,000 of a deductible temporary difference. The enacted tax rate was 25%.

Dr Deferred tax asset                                   15,000
    Cr Income tax expense—deferred                       15,000

Subsequently, Onecent Ltd. determined that only 60% of the deferred tax asset was recoverable. Which of the following journal entries should Onecent make when it determined that only 60% of the deferred tax asset was recoverable?

(1) Dr Income tax expense—current                        6,000
    Cr Income tax payable                                     6,000

(2) Dr Income tax expense—deferred                       6,000
    Cr Allowance to reduce deferred tax asset                6,000

(3) Dr Income tax expense—deferred                       6,000
    Cr Deferred tax asset                                    6,000

(4) Dr Income tax expense—deferred                       9,000
    Cr Deferred tax asset                                    9,000

(5) No journal entry is necessary.

**CHAPTER 17**

# Statement of Cash Flows

## Statement of Cash Flows

### 17-1

In which of the following categories should cash received from sales of property, plant and equipment be reported in a statement of cash flows?

(1) Financing activities
(2) Operating activities
(3) Investing activities
(4) Sales activities
(5) None of the above

### 17-2

Green Company reported profit of €115,000 in its statement of profit or loss for the year ended 31 December 20X0. The following information is available to compute its profit in 20X0.

| | |
|---|---|
| Depreciation expense | € 8,500 |
| Loss on sale of equipment | 8,230 |
| Equity income from investment in Pine Company | 12,500 |

How much should Green Company report as the net cash provided by operating activities for 20X0?

(1) €110,770
(2) €119,230
(3) €121,130
(4) €127,430
(5) €127,770

## Statement of Cash Flows

### Questions 3 through 5 are based on the following:

The following information is available for ABC Company in preparing its statement of cash flows under the indirect method for the year ended 31 December 20X2.

① On 2 January 20X2, ABC sold equipment costing $600,000 with a carrying amount of $240,000 for $260,000 cash.

② ABC purchased new equipment for a $2,000,000 note payable on 20 November 20X2. The due date of the note payable is 20 March 20X3.

③ ABC recognised a $300,000 impairment loss on securities measured at amortised cost on 31 December 20X2.

④ ABC reclassified $650,000 of long-term debt into debt due within one-year during 20X2.

⑤ ABC entered into $300,000 long-term borrowing contract with FG bank on 15 April 20X2.

⑥ ABC issued a $500,000 bond on 20 May 20X2.

⑦ During 20X2, ABC financed $3,400,000 by the issuance of ordinary shares.

⑧ ABC declared and paid $550,000 of cash dividends during 20X2.

Statement of Cash Flows

## 17-3

Based on the above information, compute the amount of the adjustment to reconcile profit to net cash provided by operating activities.

(1) $(100,000)
(2) $ 50,000
(3) $ 100,000
(4) $ 280,000
(5) $ 350,000

## 17-4

Based on the above information, compute the amount of net cash flows from investing activities.

(1) $ 240,000
(2) $ 260,000
(3) $ 600,000
(4) $2,260,000
(5) $2,600,000

## Statement of Cash Flows

### 17-5

Based on the above information, compute the amount of net cash flows from financing activities.

(1) $(3,650,000)
(2) $(3,150,000)
(3) $ 2,050,000
(4) $ 3,650,000
(5) $ 4,750,000

### 17-6

Which of the following items cannot be classified as cash flows from operating activities?

(1) Cash payments of dividends
(2) Cash payments to suppliers for goods
(3) Cash receipts from sales of goods
(4) Cash receipts of interest
(5) Cash repayments of loans

# CHAPTER 18

難易度レベル ★★★

# Business Combinations / Consolidated Statements

Bookkeeping & Accounting Test for International Communication

## BATIC
Bookkeeper & Accountant Level

## Business Combinations / Consolidated Statements

### 18-1

How should an acquirer measure non-controlling interest in an acquiree at the acquisition date?

(1) At fair value

(2) As its proportionate share of the acquiree's identifiable net assets

(3) Either at fair value or as its proportionate share of the acquiree's identifiable net assets

(4) The higher of fair value and its proportionate share of the acquiree's identifiable net assets

(5) None of the above

**Business Combinations / Consolidated Statements**

## 18-2

Select the appropriate number to fill in the following blank.

When a company invests in another company, the investing company should determine whether it should consolidate the investee by assessing whether it _____ the investee.

(1) Benefits
(2) Controls
(3) Defines
(4) Owns
(5) Supports

# Business Combinations / Consolidated Statements

## 18-3

Pixy Corporation obtained 80% of the shares of Style Incorporated by paying $1,300,000 in cash on 1 January 20X0. On the same date, the fair value of Style's assets, excluding inventory, and liabilities equaled their carrying amounts of $1,470,000 and $350,000, respectively. Inventory account had the fair value of $260,000 and the book value of $180,000. The fair value of non-controlling Interest was $280,000. Pixy chose to measure the non-controlling interest in Style as its proportionate share of the Style's identifiable net assets.

From the above information, compute the amount of goodwill that should be recorded in the consolidated statement of financial position as at 1 January 20X0.

## Business Combinations / Consolidated Statements

### Questions 4 and 5 are based on the following:

Prime Company owns 70% interest of Sun Company's ordinary shares, which was acquired early in 20X0. The following is the selected information for Prime and Sun during 20X0.

|  | Prime | Sun |
|---|---|---|
| Sales | $800,000 | $200,000 |
| Cost of sales | 490,000 | 144,000 |

During 20X0, Prime sold merchandise costing $40,000 to Sun for $50,000. At 31 December 20X0, one fourth of this merchandise still remained in Sun's inventory.

### 18-4

What amount should the consolidated sales of Prime and Sun be during 20X0?

(1) $ 950,000
(2) $ 960,000
(3) $ 987,500
(4) $ 990,000
(5) $1,000,000

## Business Combinations / Consolidated Statements

### 18-5

What amount should the consolidated cost of sales of Prime and Sun be during 20X0?

(1) $586,500
(2) $591,500
(3) $594,000
(4) $624,000
(5) $634,000

Business Combinations / Consolidated Statements

## 18-6

The following are the statements of profit or loss for Paradise Company and its 80% owned subsidiary, Son Company, for the year ended 31 December 20X0.

|  | Paradise | Son |
|---|---|---|
| Sales | $800,000 | $200,000 |
| Cost of sales | 490,000 | 144,000 |
| Gross profit | 310,000 | 56,000 |
| Expenses | 160,000 | 36,000 |
| Profit | $150,000 | $ 20,000 |

During 20X0, Son sold merchandise costing $40,000 to Paradise for $50,000. At 31 December 20X0, one fourth of this merchandise still remained in Paradise's inventory.

Compute the following amounts that should be reflected in the consolidated statement of profit or loss for 20X0.

(a) Profit to non-controlling interest
(b) Sales
(c) Cost of sales
(d) Profit to owners of the parent

Chapter 18

# Business Combinations / Consolidated Statements

## 18-7

On 1 January 20X2, P Company acquired an 80% interest in S Company in exchange for $400,000 in cash.

The fair value and book value of S Company's assets as at 1 January 20X2 are as follows.

|  | Book value | Fair value |
|---|---|---|
| Inventories | $ 30,000 | $ 40,000 |
| Buildings | 200,000 | 250,000 |
| Equipment | 100,000 | 130,000 |
| Machinery | 150,000 | 170,000 |
| Other assets | 50,000 | 70,000 |

The fair value of the non-controlling interest was $90,000 as at 1 January 20X2. P Company chose to measure the non-controlling interest in S Company at fair value.

## Business Combinations / Consolidated Statements

Prepare the elimination entries and fill up the working paper below.
The first two columns are derived from the books of P Company and S Company immediately subsequent to the acquisition.

Consolidation Working Paper at Date of Acquisition ($)

| | P Company | S Company | Adjustment and Elimination | | Non-controlling Interest | | Consolidated |
| --- | --- | --- | --- | --- | --- | --- | --- |
| | | | Dr | Cr | Dr | Cr | Balances |
| Cash | 300,000 | 50,000 | | | | | |
| Accounts receivable | 130,000 | 160,000 | | | | | |
| Inventories | 114,000 | 30,000 | | | | | |
| Buildings | 400,000 | 200,000 | | | | | |
| Equipment | 200,000 | 100,000 | | | | | |
| Machinery | 250,000 | 150,000 | | | | | |
| Investment in S | 400,000 | | | | | | |
| Investment | 0 | 100,000 | | | | | |
| Other assets | 120,000 | 50,000 | | | | | |
| Goodwill | | | | | | | |
| Total Assets | 1,914,000 | 840,000 | | | | | |
| Short-term borrowings | 120,000 | 70,000 | | | | | |
| Accounts payable | 150,000 | 95,000 | | | | | |
| Long-term debt | 100,000 | 155,000 | | | | | |
| Bonds | 320,000 | 220,000 | | | | | |
| Share capital | 700,000 | 150,000 | | | | | |
| Share premium | 200,000 | 50,000 | | | | | |
| Retained earnings | 324,000 | 100,000 | | | | | |
| Non-controlling interest | | | | | | | |
| Total Liabilities and Equity | 1,914,000 | 840,000 | | | | | |

Chapter 18

95

# Business Combinations / Consolidated Statements

## 18-8

On 1 October 20X2, Yokohama Corporation acquired 350 of Minato Company's 1,000 outstanding shares for ¥5,250,000. Minato's profit for 20X2 was ¥400,000. Assuming that goodwill is not impaired, what is the amount Yokohama should report as its investment in Minato in its 31 December 20X2 statement of financial position?

(1) ¥4,585,000
(2) ¥5,250,000
(3) ¥5,285,000
(4) ¥5,390,000
(5) ¥5,650,000

# CHAPTER 19

問題編

難易度レベル ★★★

# The Effects of Changes in Foreign Exchange Rates

Bookkeeping & Accounting Test for International Communication

# BATIC
Bookkeeper & Accountant Level

The Effects of Changes in Foreign Exchange Rates

## 19-1

A foreign subsidiary's functional currency is the currency of the country in which it is located. Its trial balance is translated from the functional currency to the presentation currency. Which exchange rate should be used for the translation of each of the following item?

(a) Cash
(b) Machinery
(c) Inventory
(d) Sales
(e) Advertising expense

① Closing rate at the date of the statement of financial position
② Exchange rate at the date of the transaction
③ Weighted-average rate for the year

## The Effects of Changes in Foreign Exchange Rates

### Questions 2 through 4 are based on the following:

An Australian subsidiary of a Japanese company was established on 1 January 20X4 by issuing shares for $80,000 cash. The subsidiary's functional and presentation currency is the Japanese yen.

During 20X4, there were the following transactions.

| Date | Transaction | Exchange rate |
|------|-------------|---------------|
| 1 January | Issued shares for $80,000 cash. | $1 = ¥92 |
| 31 March | Paid expenses with $40,000 cash. | $1 = ¥93 |
| 1 July | Performed services and received $50,000 cash. | $1 = ¥96 |
| 1 October | Performed services and received $20,000 cash. | $1 = ¥97 |
| 10 December | Purchased office equipment* for $25,000 cash. | $1 = ¥98 |
| 31 December | — | $1 = ¥95 |

\* Management chose to measure the office equipment at cost. Ignore depreciation.

### 19-2

What amount of revenue from services should be recorded in the subsidiary's statement of profit or loss for the year ended 31 December 20X4?

¥[          ]

Chapter 19

99

The Effects of Changes in Foreign Exchange Rates

## 19-3

What amount of cash should be recorded in the subsidiary's statement of financial position as at 31 December 20X4?

¥[          ]


## 19-4

What amount of profit should be recorded in the subsidiary's statement of profit or loss for the year ended 31 December 20X4?

¥[          ]

## CHAPTER 20

問題編

難易度レベル ★☆☆

# Accounting Policies, Changes in Accounting Estimates and Errors

Bookkeeping & Accounting Test for International Communication

**BATIC**

Bookkeeper & Accountant Level

## Accounting Policies, Changes in Accounting Estimates and Errors

**20-1**

Max Company adopted the FIFO method as its accounting policy for inventory valuation, using the periodic inventory system. During 20X2, Max discovered that the ending inventory values reported for 20X0 and 20X1 were incorrectly stated as follows:

20X0           €20,000 overstated

20X1           € 5,000 understated

Before any adjustment for this error, Max's 20X2 beginning balance of retained earnings would be

(1) No effect
(2) € 5,000 understated
(3) €15,000 understated
(4) €15,000 overstated
(5) None of the above

Accounting Policies, Changes in Accounting Estimates and Errors

## 20-2

During 20X0, Lax Company changed from an accounting policy, which is not in conformity with IFRSs, to the conforming one. Lax should report the effect of this change as

(1) Extraordinary item
(2) Prior year restatement resulting from changes in accounting principles
(3) Prior year restatement resulting from correction of an error
(4) Income tax
(5) None of the above

## 20-3

Tower Company purchased a machine for $500,000 with a 10-year expected useful life and no residual value on 1 January 20X0. The machine was depreciated by the straight-line method. At 1 January 20X2, Tower reestimated that this machine's useful life was 6 years from the date of acquisition and residual value was $40,000. As a result of this change, what amount of accumulated depreciation should Tower recognise for this machine at 31 December 20X2?

(1) $230,000
(2) $200,000
(3) $190,000
(4) $150,000
(5) None of the above

Accounting Policies, Changes in Accounting Estimates and Errors

## 20-4

During 20X6, Owen Corporation made a change in an accounting principle. Unless it is impracticable, Owen should:

a. Include cumulative effect of a change in accounting principle in 20X6 income statement.

b. Retrospectively apply the new accounting principle to the last period.

c. Retrospectively apply the new accounting principle to all prior periods.

(1)  a. only

(2)  b. only

(3)  c. only

(4)  a. or b. only

(5)  a. or c. only

**CHAPTER 21**

問題編

難易度レベル ★★★

# Earnings per Share

Bookkeeping & Accounting Test for International Communication

# BATIC
Bookkeeper & Accountant Level

# Earnings per Share

## 21-1

During 20X0, Jo Company had the following capital structures.

- Ordinary shares, $25 par, 4,000,000 shares outstanding

  $100,000,000
- Convertible preference shares, $15 par, non-cumulative 500,000 shares
  outstanding                                                   $7,500,000

Convertible preference shares is convertible into 1,000,000 shares of ordinary shares. For 20X0, Jo Company reported profit of $47,500,000 and declared preference dividends of $5 per share. In its 20X0 statement of comprehensive income, what amount of diluted earnings per share should Jo Company report?

(1) $ 8.50

(2) $ 9.50

(3) $11.25

(4) $12.90

(5) None of the above

Earnings per Share

**Questions 2 and 3 are based on the following:**

The following information relates to ABC Company's capital structure.

Ordinary shares
€10 par value ordinary shares
from 1 January 20X0 through 31 December 20X0          10,000 shares
Preference shares
€5 par value, 8% cumulative convertible preference shares
from 1 January 20X0 through 31 December 20X0          2,000 shares
Each share is convertible into two ordinary shares.

Profit for 20X0
€70,000

## 21-2

What amount should ABC Company report as basic earnings per share for the year ended 31 December 20X0? The amount should be rounded off to the second decimal place.

(1)  €5.00
(2)  €6.73
(3)  €6.92
(4)  €7.00
(5)  €7.08

## Earnings per Share

### 21-3

What amount should ABC Company report as diluted earnings per share for the year ended 31 December 20X0? The amount should be rounded off to the second decimal place.

(1) €5.00

(2) €6.73

(3) €6.92

(4) €7.00

(5) €7.08

# CHAPTER 22

難易度レベル ★★☆

# Interim Financial Reporting

Bookkeeping & Accounting Test for International Communication

# BATIC
Bookkeeper & Accountant Level

## Interim Financial Reporting

### 22-1

Select the most appropriate number to fill in the following blank.

A company may provide less information included in its interim financial reports as compared with its annual financial reports. One of the reasons is in the interest of ⬚ .

(1) Comparability
(2) Relevance
(3) Reliability
(4) Timeliness
(5) Verifiability

### 22-2

In January, Green Corporation planned an annual employee training programme which would incur €40,000 of costs in the second quarter. The programme was actually held in the second quarter.

What amount should be reported as expense in its respective interim statements of comprehensive income?

|     | 1st quarter | 2nd quarter | 3rd quarter | 4th quarter |
| --- | --- | --- | --- | --- |
| (1) | €0 | €0 | €20,000 | €20,000 |
| (2) | €0 | €40,000 | €0 | €0 |
| (3) | €10,000 | €10,000 | €10,000 | €10,000 |
| (4) | €20,000 | €20,000 | €0 | €0 |
| (5) | €40,000 | €0 | €0 | €0 |

# CHAPTER 23

問題編

難易度レベル ★★☆

# Operating Segments

Bookkeeping & Accounting Test for International Communication

BATIC

Bookkeeper & Accountant Level

## Operating Segments

### 23-1

The information below relates to Yellow Corporation's six operating segments.

(Yen in millions)

| Segment | Total revenue* | Intersegment revenue | Operating profit | Assets |
|---|---|---|---|---|
| A | 40 | | 20 | 10 |
| B | 120 | | 40 | 80 |
| C | 350 | 200 | 80 | 120 |
| D | 500 | 250 | (150) | 200 |
| E | 600 | 100 | 230 | 200 |
| F | 1,000 | 300 | 280 | 600 |
| Total | 2,610 | 850 | 500 | 1,210 |

* Total revenue includes intersegment revenue.

Yellow's reportable operating segments are

(1) A, B, C, D, E, and F.

(2) B, C, D, E, and F.

(3) C, D, E, and F.

(4) D, E, and F.

(5) E and F.

Operating Segments

## 23-2

The following information relates to ABC Company's six operating segments:

| Segment | Total revenue* | Intersegment revenue | Operating profit | Assets |
|---------|---------------|---------------------|------------------|--------|
| A | $10,000 | $1,000 | $300 | $10,000 |
| B | 7,000 | 1,500 | 150 | 10,000 |
| C | 5,000 | 2,000 | 120 | 3,000 |
| D | 4,000 | 2,000 | 30 | 2,000 |
| E | 2,000 | 1,500 | 50 | 1,000 |
| F | 1,000 | 500 | 50 | 500 |
| Total | $29,000 | $8,500 | $700 | $26,500 |

* Total revenue includes intersegment revenue.

How many reportable segments does ABC have?

(1) Two

(2) Three

(3) Four

(4) Five

(5) Six

問題編

## Appendix

# Time Value of Money

Bookkeeping & Accounting Test for International Communication

# BATIC
Bookkeeper & Accountant Level

# Time Value of Money

## A-1

On 30 November 20X2, James Ltd sold industrial machinery to Adams Ltd and received a non-interest-bearing note requiring 5 annual payments of $20,000. The first payment date is 30 November 20X3. The market interest rate for similar notes at date of issuance was 8%. The following is information on present value factors:

| | |
|---|---|
| Present value of $1 at 8% for 4 periods | $0.74 |
| Present value of $1 at 8% for 5 periods | 0.68 |
| Present value of an ordinary annuity of $1 at 8% for 4 periods | 3.31 |
| Present value of an ordinary annuity of $1 at 8% for 5 periods | 3.99 |

On 30 November 20X2, what amount should James report as note receivable?

(1) $66,200

(2) $71,500

(3) $79,800

(4) $86,200

(5) None of the above

# Time Value of Money

### A-2

Which of the following time value concepts will yield the largest value of $100,000 for 8% interest rate for 5 periods?

(1) Present value of an annuity due of 1 at 8% for 5 periods

(2) Future value of an ordinary annuity of 1 at 8% for 5 periods

(3) Future value of 1 at 8% for 5 periods

(4) Present value of 1 at 8% for 5 periods

(5) Present value of an ordinary annuity of 1 at 8% for 5 periods

**CHAPTER 1**

解答編

# International Financial Reporting Standards and its Conceptual Framework

Bookkeeping & Accounting Test for International Communication

# BATIC

Bookkeeper & Accountant Level

## International Financial Reporting Standards and its Conceptual Framework

### 1-1

汎用的な財務報告の主要な利用者に含まれるのは、次のうちどれか。

(1) 消費者

(2) 投資家

(3) 経営者

(4) 規制当局

(5) 上記全て

**解答　(2)**

**解説** ················································· 公式テキストChapter1-3

IFRS概念フレームワークでは、Existing and potential investors, lenders and other creditors（現在のおよび潜在的な投資者、融資者、その他の債権者）が、財務報告のPrimary users（主要な利用者）とされている。

### 1-2

有用な財務情報の基本的質的特性の一つとして正しいのは次のうちどれか。

(1) 比較可能性

(2) 目的適合性

(3) 適時性

(4) 理解可能性

(5) 検証可能性

**解答　(2)**

**解説**··············································· 公式テキストChapter1-3

有用な財務情報は、Relevance（目的適合性）とFaithful presentation（忠実な表現）の2つを基本的特性として備えていなければならない。

解答編

# CHAPTER 2

## Financial Statements

Bookkeeping & Accounting Test for International Communication

# BATIC
Bookkeeper & Accountant Level

## Financial Statements

### 2-1

ウエスト社は、20X0年12月31日に終了する年度において、継続事業からの利益 $35,000 を計上していた。さらに、ウエスト社は配当宣言をして現金配当を$9,000 おこない、また、20X0年の確定給付制度の再測定における利得が$2,000（税引後）あった。ウエスト社の 20X0年の当期純利益と包括利益を求めよ。

|     | 当期純利益 | 包括利益 |
| --- | --- | --- |
| (1) | $26,000 | $26,000 |
| (2) | $26,000 | $28,000 |
| (3) | $35,000 | $26,000 |
| (4) | $35,000 | $37,000 |
| (5) | $37,000 | $28,000 |

### 解答　(4)

**解説** ………………………………………………………………… 公式テキストChapter2-3

包括利益は、当期純利益とOther comprehensive income（その他の包括利益）の合算になる。確定給付制度の再測定は、その他の包括利益に含まれる。

Financial Statements

## 2-2

次のうち、その他の包括利益の項目として表示されるものはどれか。

a. 固定資産の再評価差益

b. 関連会社の利益に対する持分

c. 為替換算調整勘定

(1) a. のみ

(2) b. のみ

(3) c. のみ

(4) a. および b. のみ

(5) a. および c. のみ

### 解答　(5)

**解説** ………………………………………………………… 公式テキストChapter2-3

関連会社の利益に対する持分は、純損益の部に表示する。

## Financial Statements

### 2-3

20X5年1月1日、モイーズ社は、在外事業体を処分して£37,000の利得を得た。在外事業体の換算差額はその他の包括利益に認識し、資本に蓄積する。20X5年1月1日、資本に蓄積された在外事業体の換算差額の貸方残高は、£25,000だった。

加えて、モイーズ社は、20X5年1月1日に自社で使用する目的の土地を£200,000で取得した。モイーズ社は、その土地を再評価モデルで評価する。20X5年12月31日、その土地の公正価値は£208,000だった。

20X5年度のその他の包括利益の構成要素は、この2つだけである。20X5年度にモイーズ社が報告しなければならないその他の包括利益はいくらか。

(1) £ (33,000)

(2) £ (17,000)

(3) £ ( 4,000)

(4) £ 20,000

(5) £ 33,000

### 解答 (2)

解説 ·························································· 公式テキストChapter2-3

£8,000 － £25,000 ＝ －£17,000
在外事業体の財務諸表の換算から生じる為替差額は、組替調整を行う。

**CHAPTER 3**

解答編

# Fair Value Measurement

Bookkeeping & Accounting Test for International Communication

# BATIC
Bookkeeper & Accountant Level

# Fair Value Measurement

## 3-1

公正価値測定について、正しいのは次のうちどれか。

(1) 公正価値は、企業固有の測定に基づく。

(2) マーケット・アプローチは同一の資産又は負債の強制された取引により得られる価格を利用する。

(3) インカム・アプローチは過去のキャッシュ・フローを単一の将来価値に直す手法を含む。

(4) コスト・アプローチは資産の現在の用役能力を再調達するのに必要な価値に基づくものである。

(5) 上記全て

### 解答　(4)

**解説** ················································· 公式テキストChapter3-1

公正価値は、市場を基礎とした測定である。また、インカム・アプローチは、将来のキャッシュ・フローを現在価値に直す手法であり、過去のキャッシュ・フローを将来価値に直すものではない。

# Fair Value Measurement

## 3-2

以下は公正価値測定に関する文である。

a. 活発な市場における同一資産又は負債の相場価格が存在するのであれば、それをインプットとして用いるのが最も望ましい。

b. レベル2のインプットは、活発な市場における同一資産又は負債の相場価格以外の観察可能なインプットである。

c. 観察可能なインプットが存在するかどうかにかかわらず、企業はレベル3のインプットを用いることができる。

正または誤の最も適切な組合せを選択せよ。

|     | a. | b. | c. |
|-----|----|----|----|
| (1) | 正 | 正 | 正 |
| (2) | 正 | 正 | 誤 |
| (3) | 正 | 誤 | 正 |
| (4) | 誤 | 正 | 誤 |
| (5) | 誤 | 誤 | 誤 |

**解答　(2)**

**解説** ………………………………………………………………… 公式テキストChapter3-1

評価技法を用いる際は、観察可能なインプットの使用を最大化しなければならない。インプットはレベル1からレベル3までに区分されており、レベル1の優先順位が最も高く、観察可能ではないインプットの優先度が最も低い。

解答編

**CHAPTER 4**

# Cash and
# Trade Receivables

Bookkeeping & Accounting Test for International Communication

# BATIC
Bookkeeper & Accountant Level

## Cash and Trade Receivables

### 4-1

20X2年3月31日時点におけるアダム社の勘定残高は以下のようになっている。

| | |
|---|---:|
| 手持ち現金 | $ 200,000 |
| 要求払預金 | 1,300,000 |
| 20X2年3月31日に口座開設した | |
| 　満期までの預入期間が6ヵ月の定期預金 | 500,000 |
| 要求払債務でアダム社の | |
| 　現金管理の不可分の一部である当座借越 | 14,000 |

20X2年3月31日時点でのアダム社の現金および現金同等物の合計額は、

(1) $1,486,000

(2) $1,500,000

(3) $1,514,000

(4) $1,986,000

(5) $2,000,000

### 解答　(1)

**解説** ……………………………………………………… 公式テキストChapter4-1

口座開設から満期までの期間が半年の定期預金は、満期までの期間が3ヵ月を超えるため短期投資に該当する。また、要求払債務で企業の現金管理の不可分の一部となっている当座借越は、現金および現金同等物に含まれる。20X2年3月31日時点のアダム社が報告すべき正しい現金残高は $200,000 + $1,300,000 - $14,000 = $1,486,000 で、(1) が正解となる。

Cash and Trade Receivables

## 4-2

以下の情報は、20X0年度のハンソン社の売掛金に関するデータである。

| | |
|---|---:|
| 20X0年1月1日における売掛金残高 | € 90,000 |
| 20X0年度における掛売上高 | 780,000 |
| 20X0年度における返品高 | 22,000 |
| 20X0年度における貸倒損失 | 11,500 |
| 20X0年度における顧客からの代金回収額 | 630,000 |
| 20X0年12月31日時点での貸倒引当金 | 32,000 |

20X0年12月31日時点のハンソン社の売掛金勘定の正しい残高は、

(1) € 206,500

(2) € 174,500

(3) € 150,000

(4) € 58,000

(5) 上記のいずれでもない

**解答 (1)**

**解説** ························································· 公式テキストChapter4-2

T字型勘定を使って売掛金勘定の動きを見ると以下のようになる。

| Accounts Receivable | | | |
|---|---:|---:|---|
| 1/1/20X0 | 90,000 | | |
| Credit sales | 780,000 | | |
| | | 22,000 | Sales returns |
| | | 11,500 | Write-offs |
| | | 630,000 | Collections |
| 31/12/20X0 | 206,500 | | |

貸倒引当金勘定の動きは売掛金勘定には影響を与えない。よって、20X0年12月31日時点でのハンソン社の売掛金残高は€ 206,500となる。

131

# Cash and Trade Receivables

## 4-3

以下の情報は20X0年12月31日時点でのジェシー社の売掛金に関する引当マトリックスである。

| 延滞期間 | グロスの帳簿価額 | 貸倒率 |
|---|---|---|
| 延滞なし | $180,000 | 1% |
| 1-30日 | 120,000 | 3% |
| 31-60日 | 90,000 | 6% |
| 60日超 | 15,000 | 25% |

20X0年12月31日時点での貸倒引当金の残高はいくら計上すべきか。

(1) $ 9,500

(2) $12,000

(3) $14,550

(4) $18,000

(5) 上記のいずれでもない

**解答　(3)**

**解説** …………………………………………………… 公式テキストChapter4-2

引当マトリックスを用いて計上すべき貸倒引当金の残高を求めると、以下のようになる。

$$
\begin{aligned}
180,000 \times 1\% &= \$ 1,800 \\
120,000 \times 3\% &= 3,600 \\
90,000 \times 6\% &= 5,400 \\
15,000 \times 25\% &= \underline{3,750} \\
&\phantom{=} \underline{\$14,550}
\end{aligned}
$$

よって、20X0年12月31日時点で、ジェシー社が計上すべき貸倒引当金残高は (3) の $14,550 となる。

解答編

# CHAPTER 5

Inventories

Bookkeeping & Accounting Test for International Communication

# BATIC
Bookkeeper & Accountant Level

# Inventories

### 5-1

パディー社は20X4年2月1日に商品を仕入れた。以下の情報は、この商品仕入れに際しパディー社に発生したコストの内訳である。

| | |
|---|---:|
| 購入代価 | £500,000 |
| 運送費 | 18,000 |
| 仕入値引き | 400 |
| 商品を仕入れるための銀行借入金利息 | 250 |

銀行借入金利息は、適格資産である当該商品の取得に直接起因するものであった。パディー社は、20X4年2月1日以前には、棚卸資産を持っていなかったと仮定する。パディー社がこれらの取引を記帳し終わった際、パディー社の棚卸資産にはいくらの残高があるか。

(1) £500,000

(2) £517,600

(3) £517,850

(4) £525,150

(5) 上記のいずれでもない

## 解答 (3)

**解説** ································································· 公式テキストChapter5-2

購入代価や運送費など、棚卸資産の取得に直接関係するコストは全て棚卸資産の原価に含まれる。また、棚卸資産が適格資産である場合、その取得に直接起因する借入コストを取得原価に含める。一方、仕入値引きは取得原価から控除する。よって、パディー社の棚卸資産は、£517,850（£500,000 + £18,000 + £250 − £400= £517,850）となる。

## Inventories

### 5-2

以下の情報は、テキサス社の20X0年3月における取引に関するものである。

| 日付 | 取引内容 | 数量 | 単価 | 合計 | 数量残高 |
|------|----------|------|------|------|----------|
| 1/3/20X0 | 残高 | 400 | $2 | $ 800 | 400 |
| 7/3/20X0 | 仕入 | 400 | 4 | 1,600 | 800 |
| 17/3/20X0 | 売上 | 600 | | | 200 |
| 22/3/20X0 | 仕入 | 800 | 5 | 4,000 | 1,000 |
| 26/3/20X0 | 売上 | 300 | | | 700 |

テキサス社は継続記録法を適用している。移動平均法をもちいた場合、テキサス社は20X0年3月31日時点の棚卸資産をいくら計上すべきか。

(1) $2,100

(2) $3,220

(3) $4,550

(4) $5,000

(5) 上記のいずれでもない

### 解答 (2)

### 解説 ···················································· 公式テキストChapter5-3

移動平均法は、商品の仕入の都度、加重平均単価を計算する方法である。20X0年3月7日の仕入によって、商品の単価は、$3(($1,600+$800)÷800個=$3)となる。3月17日の売上で棚卸資産は、$600($3×200個)となり、3月22日の仕入後の単価は、$4.6(($600+$4,000)÷1,000個=$4.6)となる。よって、3月26日の売上後の棚卸資産は、$3,220($4.6×700)となる。

## Inventories

### 5-3

以下の情報は、ある会計年度におけるABC社が保有する棚卸資産に関連する情報である。

|  | 商品 A | 商品 B | 商品 C |
|---|---|---|---|
| 数量 | 700 | 500 | 800 |
| 単位当たりの取得原価 | $ 80 | $ 95 | $ 60 |
| 単位当たりの再調達原価 | $ 70 | $ 90 | $ 55 |
| 単位当たりの見積り販売価格 | $ 90 | $100 | $ 75 |
| 単位当たりの見積り販売費用 | $ 15 | $ 20 | $ 10 |

当該会計期末の財務諸表において、ABC社が棚卸資産として報告すべき金額はいくらか。

(1) $133,000

(2) $138,000

(3) $140,500

(4) $144,500

(5) $151,500

解答 (3)

解説 ............................................................ 公式テキストChapter5-3

商品A：取得原価［$80］＞ 正味実現可能価額［$90 − $15 = $75］

商品B：取得原価［$95］＞ 正味実現可能価額［$100 − $20 = $80］

商品C：取得原価［$60］＜ 正味実現可能価額［$75 − $10 = $65］

700 × $75 + 500 × $80 + 800 × $60 = $140,500

# Inventories

## 5-4

棚卸資産の評価に関する以下の文章のうち、適切ではないものはどれか。

(1) 棚卸資産の原価を算定する方法として、LIFO を使用することはできない。

(2) 棚卸資産の評価減は正味実現可能価額が増加する明白な証拠があれば、戻し入れることができる。

(3) 棚卸資産の原価が回収不可能な場合は、原価を正味実現可能価額まで切り下げる。

(4) 棚卸資産の原価の回収可能性は、原価と公正価値を比較することによって測定される。

(5) 個別法は、通常代替性がなく、特定のプロジェクトのために区分されている項目に適切である。

**解答　(4)**

**解説** ……………………………………………………………………… 公式テキストChapter5-3

棚卸資産の原価とその正味実現可能価額を比較して、正味実現可能価額が原価を下回っている場合に評価減を計上する。正味実現可能価額は企業固有の価額だが、公正価値は第三者による取引によって決定される価額なので、棚卸資産の正味実現可能価額と公正価値は一致しないことがある。

**CHAPTER 6**

解答編

# Property, Plant and Equipment

Bookkeeping & Accounting Test for International Communication

# BATIC

Bookkeeper & Accountant Level

## Property, Plant and Equipment

### 6-1

20X4年1月1日、ジャクソン社は、業務上必要になったため機械を $72,000で購入した。この機械に関して、20X4年に発生した費用は以下のとおりである。

| | |
|---|---:|
| 購入時の輸送費 | $3,600 |
| 意図した使用の場所に機械を運んで据え付けるためにかかった費用 | 2,900 |
| 意図した使用が可能な状態になるまでの間に行った、機械が正常に働くかどうかのテストにかかった費用 | 4,400 |
| 意図した使用が可能な状態になった後に行った、機械が正常に働くかどうかのテストにかかった費用 | 2,700 |
| 日常的な機械の維持費用 | 1,500 |

ジャクソン社は、この機械の取得原価をいくらで記帳すべきか。

(1) $75,600

(2) $82,900

(3) $84,400

(4) $85,600

(5) $87,100

### 解答　(2)

**解説** ································································· 公式テキスト Chapter6-2

有形固定資産の取得原価に算入するのは、その資産を経営者が意図した方法で稼働可能にするために必要な場所と状態に置くことに直接起因するコストである。また、保守や修繕に関わる日常的なコストは取得原価に含めない。よって、この機械の取得原価は $82,900（$72,000 + $3,600 + $2,900 + $4,400 = $82,900）となる。

140

Property, Plant and Equipment

問題2および3は以下に基づく。

20X5年1月1日、ファーガソン社は自社工場の建設を始め、そのために、銀行より5%の利息で£200,000の借り入れを行った。ファーガソン社は、工事期間は16か月と見込んでいる。建設に関する上記の借入に加えて、20X5年にファーガソン社には以下の負債があった。

20X3年1月1日発行の年利8%、5年満期の社債。利息は毎年支払う。　　　£180,000
20X4年1月1日に振り出した年利6%、3年満期の手形。利息は毎年支払う。　　120,000

20X5年にファーガソン社が当該建設のために支払った金額は次の通りである。

　1月1日　£200,000
10月1日　　100,000

### 6-2

ファーガソン社は資産化率を適用する支出の合理的な近似値として、加重平均累積支出額を用いている。20X5年における工場への支出額を計算しなさい。

(1) £100,000

(2) £200,000

(3) £225,000

(4) £300,000

(5) 上記のいずれでもない

解答　(3)

解説 ………………………………………………………………… 公式テキスト Chapter6-2

£200,000 × 12/12 + £100,000 × 3/12 = £225,000

**141**

## Property, Plant and Equipment

### 6-3

20X5年に資産化すべき利息を計算しなさい。

(1) £10,000

(2) £11,250

(3) £11,800

(4) £26,200

(5) £31,600

**解答 (3)**

解説 ⋯⋯⋯⋯⋯⋯⋯⋯⋯⋯⋯⋯⋯⋯⋯⋯⋯⋯⋯⋯⋯⋯⋯ 公式テキスト Chapter6-2

工場を建設するために銀行から借り入れた£200,000の借入コスト（£200,000 × 5% ＝£10,000）を資産化する。一般目的で借り入れた社債£180,000と手形£120,000については、工場を建設するために使用した範囲（£225,000［加重平均支出額］－£200,000［工場を建設するための借入資金］＝£25,000）で借入コストを資産化する。

また、資産化率は次のように計算される。

| | 元本 | 利息 |
|---|---|---|
| 年利8%、5年満期の社債 | £180,000 | £14,400 |
| 年利6%、3年満期の手形 | 120,000 | 7,200 |
| | £300,000 | £21,600 |

資産化率＝£21,600÷£300,000 ＝ 7.2%

資産化する借入コスト：£11,800（£10,000＋£25,000×7.2% ＝£11,800）

## Property, Plant and Equipment

### 6-4

スパレッティ社は€60,000で購入したトラックを保有している。20X3年12月31日、同社はそのトラックのタイヤを原価€8,000の新しいタイヤと取替え、取替え後、新しいタイヤに€7,000を支払った。

そのトラックに関して、スパレッティ社は、重要な構成要素を基礎に会計記録の保存と減価償却を行っている。以下は、20X3年12月31日におけるトラックの重要な構成要素に関する情報である。

|  | 取得原価 | 減価償却累計額 |
|---|---|---|
| エンジンとトランスミッション | €15,000 | € 7,800 |
| 車体構造 | 36,000 | 12,000 |
| タイヤ | 9,000 | 6,000 |

タイヤの取替えについてスパレッティ社が記録すべき損益はいくらか。

**解答　€2,000の損失**

**解説** ………………………………………………………………… 公式テキスト Chapter6-2

| | | |
|---|---|---|
| Dr Tyres（truck） | 8,000 | |
| 　Accumulated depreciation — Tyres | 6,000 | |
| 　Loss on disposal of tyres | 2,000 | |
| Cr Tyres（truck） | | 9,000 |
| 　Cash | | 7,000 |

## Property, Plant and Equipment

### 6-5

XYZ 社は、事業に使用する目的で土地を所有している。会計期間のはじめ、その土地の帳簿価額は $750,000 で、再評価剰余金の貸方残高が $12,000 あった。同会計期間末、その土地の公正価値は、鑑定によって $730,000 と決定された。XYZ 社は、その土地に対して再評価モデルを使用している。その土地に対する再評価の結果として、XYZ 社がその他の包括利益に計上すべき損失の額はいくらか。

(1) $0

(2) $ 8,000

(3) $12,000

(4) $20,000

(5) $32,000

**解答　(3)**

**解説** ⋯⋯⋯⋯⋯⋯⋯⋯⋯⋯⋯⋯⋯⋯⋯⋯⋯⋯⋯⋯⋯⋯ 公式テキスト Chapter6-3

> 公正価値への再評価において帳簿価額が減少する場合、まず過去の再評価において認識した再評価剰余金の貸方残高をその残高の範囲内で取り崩し、その他の包括利益に計上する。よって、帳簿価額 $750,000 と公正価値 $730,000 の差額 $20,000 のうち、再評価剰余金 $12,000 をその他の包括利益に計上し、残額の $8,000 を当期の損失として計上する。

Property, Plant and Equipment

## 6-6

20X0年11月1日に、ABC社は古い設備をXYZ社に$100,000で売却した。設備の取得価額は$150,000で、残存価額は$15,000であった。20X0年11月1日現在の減価償却累計額は$54,000だった。ABCは売却損益をいくら認識すべきか。

(1) $( 19,000)

(2) $ 0

(3) $  4,000

(4) $  11,000

(5) $ 100,000

解答　(3)

解説 ………………………………………………………… 公式テキスト Chapter6-4

以下のような仕訳がなされる。

| | | |
|---|---|---|
| Dr Cash | 100,000 | |
| Accumulated depreciation | 54,000 | |
| Cr Equipment | | 150,000 |
| Gain on sale | | 4,000（差額） |

145

# Property, Plant and Equipment

問題7および8は以下に基づく。

大宮花店は2つの建物を持っている。経営陣はこれらの建物を売却することを決定し、使用目的保有の資産から売却目的保有の資産へと分類を変更しようとしている。

## 6-7

次のうち、大宮が分類を変更できない状況はどれか。

(1) 2つの建物は現在の状態ですぐにも売却可能である。
(2) 大宮はすでに不動産雑誌に売却の広告を掲載し始めた。
(3) 大宮は10ヵ月後には売却は完了すると予測している。
(4) もし10ヵ月後に売れていなければ、大宮は計画を撤回するつもりである。
(5) 上記のいずれでもない。

### 解答　(4)

解説······················································· 公式テキスト Chapter6-5

建物を売却する可能性が非常に高く（highly probable）なければ、売却目的保有に分類変更できない。売却の可能性が非常に高いと言えるためには、売却計画を完了させるために必要な行動が、計画を撤回する可能性が低い（unlikely）ことを示している必要がある。

Property, Plant and Equipment

## 6-8

20X7年7月1日に、売却予定の2件が販売目的資産に分類された。

| | 取得日 | 取得原価 | 残存価額 | 償却期間 | 1/7/20X7 売却コスト控除後の 公正価値 | 減価償却 方法 |
|---|---|---|---|---|---|---|
| 建物A | 1/1/20X0 | ¥1,000,000 | ¥10,000 | 9年 | ¥400,000 | 定額法 |
| 建物B | 1/7/20X2 | ¥1,200,000 | ¥100,000 | 10年 | ¥490,000 | 定額法 |

この状況に基づき、分類に関連して必要となる仕訳を行いなさい。
建物の分類変更のための仕訳は無視する。

(1) 仕訳なし

(2) (借方) 減価償却費　　　　　　　110,000
　　　　 (貸方) 減価償却累計額　　　　　　　　　　　110,000
　　 (借方) 減損損失　　　　　　　　160,000
　　　　 (貸方) 固定資産　　　　　　　　　　　　　　160,000

(3) (借方) 減価償却費　　　　　　　220,000
　　　　 (貸方) 減価償却累計額　　　　　　　　　　　220,000
　　 (借方) 減損損失　　　　　　　　105,000
　　　　 (貸方) 固定資産　　　　　　　　　　　　　　105,000

(4) (借方) 減損損失　　　　　　　　215,000
　　　　 (貸方) 固定資産　　　　　　　　　　　　　　215,000

(5) (借方) 減価償却費　　　　　　　220,000
　　　　 (貸方) 減価償却累計額　　　　　　　　　　　220,000

147

## 解答 （2）

解説 ·················································· 公式テキスト Chapter6-5

| | 1/1/20X7の | | 1/7/20X7 | | |
| --- | --- | --- | --- | --- | --- |
| | 簿価 | 上期償却 | 簿価 | 公正価値 | 減損損失 |
| 建物A | ¥230,000 | ¥55,000 | ¥175,000 | ¥400,000 | ¥0 |
| 建物B | 705,000 | 55,000 | 650,000 | 490,000 | 160,000 |

分類変更の直前にそれぞれの帳簿価額を測定し、売却コスト控除後の公正価値と比較する。

建物Bは、20X7年7月1日時点の簿価が公正価値を上回っているため、減損損失¥160,000を認識しなければならない。

売却目的に分類変更された資産は、簿価か公正価値のうち低い方で記載され、以後、減価償却は中止する。

解答編

# CHAPTER 7

## Intangible Assets

Bookkeeping & Accounting Test for International Communication

# BATIC
Bookkeeper & Accountant Level

## Intangible Assets

## 7-1

次の空欄に最も適切な組み合わせを選びなさい。

企業がある項目を無形資産として認識する場合、その項目は過去の出来事の結果として企業に [ A ] いて、なおかつのれんと区別するために [ B ] であることが要求される。そしてさらに、その項目から企業に [ C ] の流入が見込まれることが要求される。

| | A | B | C |
|---|---|---|---|
| (1) | 認証されて | 代替的 | 現金および現金同等物 |
| (2) | 認証されて | 識別可能 | 将来の経済的便益 |
| (3) | 支配されて | 代替的 | 現金および現金同等物 |
| (4) | 支配されて | 識別可能 | 将来の経済的便益 |
| (5) | 支配されて | 識別可能 | 現金および現金同等物 |

### 解答　(4)

解説 ································································ 公式テキスト Chapter7-2

無形資産を認識するには、認識しようとする項目の取得または自己創設において発生したコストが、無形資産の定義と認識規準の両方を満たしていなければならない。

150

# Intangible Assets

## 7-2

ロサリオ社は新しい製品の開発中である。開発中の製品に関して、20X5年1月1日から20X5年8月31日までの間に€250,000、20X5年9月1日から20X5年12月31日までの間に€17,000の支出があった。ロサリオ社は、20X5年9月1日に開発中の製品が無形資産の認識要件を満たしたことを証明することができる。20X5年度の財務諸表において費用および資産としていくら認識しなければならないか。

|  | 費用 | 資産 |
|---|---|---|
| (1) | €0 | €0 |
| (2) | €250,000 | €0 |
| (3) | €267,000 | €0 |
| (4) | €250,000 | €17,000 |
| (5) | €0 | €267,000 |

### 解答　(4)

**解説** ································································ 公式テキスト Chapter7-2

無形資産を認識するための要件を最初に満たした日以降に発生した支出は、資産として認識しなければならない。

Chapter 7

151

## Intangible Assets

### 7-3

20X0年1月1日に、スミス社は£500,000でベストセラー小説の著作権を取得した。また20X0年に、同社は著作権登録のために£20,000の弁護士費用を支払った。この著作権の契約上の権利は50年である。著作権の将来の経済的便益が消費されるパターンは、信頼性をもって決定することができない。第三者による著作権の購入契約や、著作権の活発な市場は存在しない。スミス社は、原価モデルを使用して著作権の会計処理を行う。

20X0年12月31日付損益計算書でスミス社の著作権に関する償却費をいくら計上すべきか。

(1) £10,000

(2) £10,400

(3) £12,500

(4) £13,000

(5) 上記のいずれでもない

### 解答　(2)

**解説** ………………………………………………………… 公式テキスト Chapter7-3

£500,000 + £20,000（法律費用）を資産計上し、50年間で償却するので、20X0年の償却費は£520,000÷50年＝£10,400となる。

# Intangible Assets

## 7-4

20X0年1月1日にパーク社はシェル社を取得し、€50,000ののれんを認識した。
20X0年12月31日に年1回の減損テストを行い、減損の兆候は認められなかった。

20X0年におけるのれんの償却費を計算せよ。

**解答**　€0

**解説** ⋯⋯⋯⋯⋯⋯⋯⋯⋯⋯⋯⋯⋯⋯⋯⋯⋯⋯⋯⋯⋯⋯ 公式テキスト Chapter7-4

のれんは償却せず、最低年1回の減損テストを行い、減損が発生したら、減損
損失額を計上する。

解答編

# CHAPTER 8

## Impairment of Property, Plant and Equipment and Intangible Assets

Bookkeeping & Accounting Test for International Communication

# BATIC

Bookkeeper & Accountant Level

Impairment of Property, Plant and Equipment and Intangible Assets

## 8-1

資産の減損に関する次の文章のうち、誤っているのはどれか。

(1) 回収可能価額は、資産の公正価値から売却費用を引いた金額と使用価値のいずれか高い方である。

(2) 個別の資産ごとに回収可能価額を見積もることができない場合は、その資産が属する資金生成単位について回収可能価額を見積もる。

(3) 以前認識した減損損失の戻し入れは認められていない。

(4) 原価モデルを選択している場合、減損損失は純損益に認識される。

(5) 資産の帳簿価額がその回収可能価額を上回っている場合、その差額が減損損失として認識される。


### 解答　(3)

**解説** ················································· 公式テキスト Chapter8-5

減損が存在していない、または減少している兆候がある場合は回収可能価額を見積もる。そして、回収可能価額の算定に使用する見積りが最後に減損損失を認識したときの見積りから変化している場合、減損損失の戻入れを行う。

## Impairment of Property, Plant and Equipment and Intangible Assets

**8-2**

20X2年1月1日に、宮崎㈱は事業のため $60,000 の機械を購入した。機械は定額法により、残存価値ゼロ、経済耐用年数5年に渡り償却される。20X2年12月31日、減損テストを行った結果、予測される将来キャッシュフローの現在価値が $30,000 しかなかった。20X2年12月31日における機械の処分コスト控除後の公正価値は $25,000 であった。20X2年12月31日、宮崎㈱はいくら減損損失を認識すべきか。

(1) $12,000

(2) $18,000

(3) $20,000

(4) $30,000

(5) $40,000

**解答　(2)**

**解説** ················································· 公式テキスト Chapter8-3, 4

資産の帳簿価額：$48,000（$60,000 − $60,000÷5 = $48,000）

使用価値（資産から生じると見込まれる将来キャッシュ・フローの現在価値）：$30,000

処分コスト控除後の公正価値：$25,000

よって減損損失は $18,000（$48,000 − $30,000 = $18,000）となる。

# Impairment of Property, Plant and Equipment and Intangible Assets

<u>問題3および4は以下に基づく。</u>

20X4年12月31日、バルデス社は、減損の兆候があった設備の減損テストを行った。設備の残存耐用年数は、20X4年12月31日時点で2年だった。次のデータは、各残存年における設備の使用と処分から生じる可能性があるキャッシュ・フローに関連している。

| 年 | 生じる可能性がある<br>キャッシュ・フロー | 確率 |
|------|------|------|
| 20X5 | € 40,000 | 20% |
| | 80,000 | 50% |
| | 90,000 | 30% |
| 20X6 | € 20,000 | 30% |
| | 40,000 | 60% |
| | 60,000 | 10% |

バルデス社は、期待キャッシュ・フロー技法を用いて設備の将来キャッシュ・フローを見積る。また、適切な割引率を7％と算定した。

## 8-3

20X5年の設備の将来キャッシュ・フローを計算せよ。

(1) €40,000

(2) €70,000

(3) €75,000

(4) €80,000

(5) €90,000

## Impairment of Property, Plant and Equipment and Intangible Assets

### 解答　(3)

**解説** ……………………………………………………… 公式テキスト Chapter8-3

€ 40,000×20％ ＋€ 80,000×50％ ＋€ 90,000×30％ ＝€ 75,000

期待キャッシュ・フロー技法では、生じうるすべての将来キャッシュ・フローの確率加重平均によって将来キャッシュ・フローを算定する。

---

### 8-4

設備の使用価値を計算せよ。必要であれば、１ドル未満は四捨五入せよ。

(1)　€  96,952

(2)　€101,537

(3)　€104,813

(4)　€111,000

(5)　€120,000

### 解答　(2)

**解説** ……………………………………………………… 公式テキスト Chapter8-3

€75,000 ÷ (1 + 0.07) + (€20,000 × 30％ + €40,000 × 60％ + €60,000 × 10％) ÷ (1 + 0.07)$^2$ ≒ €101,537

将来キャッシュ・フローの現在価値が使用価値となる。

Chapter 8

## 8-5

20X4年1月1日、スパルタン社は耐用年数5年、残存価額¥0の設備¥5,000,000を購入した。スパルタン社は、その設備を原価モデルで測定し、定額法で減価償却を行う。20X5年12月31日、事業環境の悪化により、スパルタン社は¥600,000の設備の減損損失を認識した。20X6年12月31日、事業環境が改善し、設備の回収可能価額を¥1,700,000と算定した。20X6年12月31日にスパルタン社が減価償却後の設備に関して行わなければならない仕訳は以下のどれか。

(1) （借方）減価償却累計額および減損損失累計額　　1,100,000
　　（貸方）その他の包括利益　　　　　　　　　　　　　　　　1,100,000

(2) （借方）減価償却累計額および減損損失累計額　　100,000
　　（貸方）減損損失の戻入れ　　　　　　　　　　　　　　　　100,000

(3) （借方）減価償却累計額および減損損失累計額　　600,000
　　（貸方）減損損失の戻入れ　　　　　　　　　　　　　　　　600,000

(4) （借方）その他の包括利益　　300,000
　　（貸方）再評価剰余金　　　　　　　　　　　　　　　　　　300,000

(5) 仕訳の必要はない。

## Impairment of Property, Plant and Equipment and Intangible Assets

## 解答 （2）

**解説** ···················································· 公式テキスト Chapter8-4,5

20X4年と20X5年の減価償却費：¥1,000,000（¥5,000,000÷5 = ¥1,000,000）

20X4年12月31日の帳簿価額：¥4,000,000（¥5,000,000 − ¥1,000,000 = ¥4,000,000）

20X5年12月31日の帳簿価額：¥2,400,000（¥4,000,000 − ¥1,000,000 −減損損失 ¥600,000 = ¥2,400,000）

20X6年の減価償却費：¥800,000（¥2,400,000÷3 = ¥800,000）

20X6年12月31日の帳簿価額（戻入れ前）：¥1,600,000（¥2,400,000 − ¥800,000 = ¥1,600,000）

よって、戻入れの金額は¥100,000（¥1,700,000 − ¥1,600,000 = ¥100,000）

### 8-6

ファーガソン社には、ユニット X、ユニット Y、ユニット Z の 3 つの資金生成単位がある。20x6 年 12 月 31 日、ファーガソン社が活動する市場環境に悪い方向への変化が見られたので、各資金生成単位について減損テストを行った。X、Y、Z の帳簿価額は、それぞれ€120,000、€180,000、€300,000 である。これらの金額にのれんは含まれない。

各資金生成単位の資産は次のようになっている。

| | ユニット X | ユニット Y | ユニット Z |
|---|---|---|---|
| 施設 | €70,000 | €112,500 | €187,500 |
| 土地 | 50,000 | 67,500 | 112,500 |

各資金生成単位の回収可能価額は以下のとおりである。

| | |
|---|---|
| ユニット X | €160,000 |
| ユニット Y | 210,000 |
| ユニット Z | 340,000 |

ファーガソン社は、そのほかにも本社と研究センターの 2 つの全社資産を所有している。本社と研究センターの帳簿価額は、それぞれ€150,000 と€90,000 である。資金生成単位の帳簿価額の比は、本社の帳簿価額の合理的な配分比率をあらわしている。研究センターの帳簿価額は、合理的な基準で 3 つの資金生成単位に配分することができない。

減損損失配分後の各全社資産の帳簿価額を計算せよ。必要であれば、小数点第一位を四捨五入せよ。

Impairment of Property, Plant and Equipment and Intangible Assets

解答　本社：€125,823　研究センター：€80,886

解説 ……………………………………………………… 公式テキスト Chapter8-4

1. 本社の帳簿価額を、各資金生成単位の帳簿価額に基づいて比例配分する。

| | 帳簿価額 | 本社の帳簿価額の配分 | 配分後の帳簿価額 |
|---|---|---|---|
| ユニット X | €120,000 | €150,000 × €120,000/€600,000 = €30,000 | €150,000 |
| ユニット Y | 180,000 | 150,000 × 180,000/ 600,000 = 45,000 | 225,000 |
| ユニット Z | 300,000 | 150,000 × 300,000/ 600,000 = 75,000 | 375,000 |

2. 各資金生成単位について、本社の帳簿価額配分後の帳簿価額と回収可能価額を比較する。

| | 本社の帳簿価額配分後の帳簿価額 | 回収可能価額 | 減損損失 |
|---|---|---|---|
| ユニット X | €150,000 | €160,000 | €0 |
| ユニット Y | 225,000 | 210,000 | 15,000 |
| ユニット Z | 375,000 | 340,000 | 35,000 |

3. ユニット Y とユニット Z について、減損損失を資産に配分する。

ユニット Y

| | 減損損失 | 減損損失配分後の帳簿価額 |
|---|---|---|
| 施設 | € 7,500（€15,000 × €112,500/€225,000） | €105,000（€112,500 − €7,500） |
| 土地 | 4,500（ 15,000 × 67,500/ 225,000） | 63,000（ 67,500 − 4,500） |
| 本社 | 3,000（ 15,000 × 45,000/ 225,000） | 42,000（ 45,000 − 3,000） |
| 合計 | €15,000 | €210,000 |

ユニット Z

| | 減損損失 | 減損損失配分後の帳簿価額 |
|---|---|---|
| 施設 | €17,500（€35,000 × €187,500/€375,000） | €170,000（€187,500 − €17,500） |
| 土地 | 10,500（ 35,000 × 112,500/ 375,000） | 102,000（ 112,500 − 10,500） |
| 本社 | 7,000（ 35,000 × 75,000/ 375,000） | 68,000（ 75,000 − 7,000） |
| 合計 | €35,000 | €340,000 |

Chapter 8

4. 研究センターの帳簿価額は合理的な基準で各資金生成単位に配分できないので、研究センターを含む最小の資金生成単位グループ（この場合はファーガソン社全体）を基礎に減損テストを行う。

| | |
|---|---|
| ユニット X | €120,000 |
| ユニット Y | 168,000（105,000+63,000） |
| ユニット Z | 272,000（170,000+102,000） |
| 本社 | 140,000（30,000+42,000+68,000） |
| 研究センター | 90,000 |
| ファーガソン社全体の帳簿価額 | 790,000 |
| ファーガソン社全体の回収可能価額 | 710,000（160,000+210,000+340,000） |
| 減損損失 | € 80,000 |

5. 減損損失をファーガソン社全体の資産に配分する。

| | 帳簿価額 | 減損損失 | 減損損失配分後の帳簿価額 |
|---|---|---|---|
| ユニット X | | | |
| 施設 | € 70,000 | € 7,089（€80,000×€ 70,000/€790,000） | € 62,911 |
| 土地 | 50,000 | 5,063（ 80,000× 50,000/ 790,000） | 44,937 |
| ユニット Y | | | |
| 施設 | 105,000 | 10,633（ 80,000× 105,000/ 790,000） | 94,367 |
| 土地 | 63,000 | 6,380（ 80,000× 63,000/ 790,000） | 56,620 |
| ユニット Z | | | |
| 施設 | 170,000 | 17,215（ 80,000× 170,000/ 790,000） | 152,785 |
| 土地 | 102,000 | 10,329（ 80,000× 102,000/ 790,000） | 91,671 |
| 本社 | 140,000 | 14,177（ 80,000× 140,000/ 790,000） | 125,823 |
| 研究センター | 90,000 | 9,114（ 80,000× 90,000/ 790,000） | 80,886 |
| | €790,000 | €80,000 | €710,000 |

解答編

# CHAPTER 9

## Lease

Bookkeeping & Accounting Test for International Communication

# BATIC
Bookkeeper & Accountant Level

# Lease

**問題1から3は以下に基づく。**

ウエスト社(借手)はアーバン社(貸手)と新しい機器に関してリース契約を締結した。情報は以下のとおりである。

| | | |
|---|---|---|
| リース開始日 | | 20X1年12月31日 |
| リース期間 | | 5年 |
| 毎期末の支払リース料 | | $2,500 |
| 見積耐用年数 | | 9年 |
| ウエスト社の追加借入利子率 | | 12% |
| ウエスト社が知っているリースの計算利子率 | | 10% |
| 5期間の期末年金の現在価値 | 10% | 3.791 |
| | 12% | 3.605 |

リース契約は更新オプションを含むものではなく、リース機器の所有権はリース契約終了時にアーバン社からウエスト社に移転するものとする。リース機器の簿価はアーバン社の帳簿上で$6,500であった。

## Lease

### 9-1

20X1年12月31日現在、ウエスト社の財政状態計算書上に計上されるリース負債の金額を求めよ。必要があれば、小数点以下は四捨五入せよ。

解答　$9,478

解説 ················································· 公式テキスト Chapter9-3

リース開始日に財政状態計算書上に計上されるリース負債およびリース資産の金額はリース料の現在価値である。割引率はリースの計算利子率が適用されるため、本問では10%で割り引かれる。設問では毎年期末のリース料の支払い$2,500以外リース料に含まれるものがないため、$2,500×3.791 ≒ $9,478が正解となる。

### 9-2

ウエスト社の20X2年の損益計算書に計上される減価償却費の金額を求めよ。ウエスト社の減価償却の方法は定額法で残存価額をゼロとする。必要があれば、小数点以下は四捨五入せよ。

解答　$1,053

解説 ················································· 公式テキスト Chapter9-3

本問ではリース契約終了時に所有権の移転が認められるため、償却期間は耐用年数の9年になる。

よって減価償却費は$9,478÷9年 ≒ $1,053になる。

# Lease

### 9-3

リース開始日におけるアーバン社の以下の仕訳の空欄を埋めよ。

(借方) リース未収金 　　　[　　　　　]
　　　 (貸方) 売上 　　　　　　　　[　　　　　　]

(借方) 売上原価 　　　　[　　　　　]
　　　 (貸方) 棚卸資産 　　　　　　[　　　　　　]

**解答**　**Dr Lease receivable**　　　**[9,478]**
　　　　**Cr Sales**　　　　　　　　　　**[9,478]**

　　　　**Dr Cost of sales**　　　　**[6,500]**
　　　　**Cr Inventory**　　　　　　　　**[6,500]**

**解説** ················································· 公式テキスト Chapter9-4

設問に Carrying amount of the leased equipment についての記述があることから、アーバン社は「製造業者または販売業者である貸手」であることが分かる。

本問では、リース料の現在価値で売上及びリース未収金（リース債権）を計上することになる。また、売上原価および棚卸資産（リースに供される資産）も認識しなければならない。なお、無保証残存価値については、この設問では記載がないので考慮する必要はないが、仮にあれば、その現在価値分を Lease receivable に増額し、同額を Cost of sales から減額する。

**Lease**

<u>問題 4 から 6 は以下に基づく。</u>

XYZ 社はリース会社から新設備をリースした。条件には、リース期間終了後の割安購入選択権、所有権の移転が含まれていない。リースに関する追加情報は次のとおりである。

| | |
|---|---:|
| リース開始日 | 20X0 年 1 月 1 日 |
| リース期間 | 8 年 |
| 年度末の年間のリース料支払い額 | $1,200 |
| 設備の公正価値 | $6,402 |
| 設備の見積耐用年数 | 10 年 |
| XYZ 社の追加借入利子率 | 11% |
| XYZ 社が知っている貸手のリースの計算利子率 | 10% |
| | |
| 減価償却 | 定額法（残存価額ゼロ） |
| | |
| 8 期間の期末年金の現在価値 | 10%　　5.335 |
| | 11%　　5.146 |

金額は小数点以下を四捨五入せよ。

### 9-4

20X0 年 12 月 31 日に終了する年度に XYZ 社が認識すべき支払利息はいくらか。

(1) $640

(2) $679

(3) $704

(4) $960

(5) $1,200

**解答　(1)**

**解説** ・・・・・・・・・・・・・・・・・・・・・・・・・・・・・・・・・・・・・・・・・・・・・・・・・・・・・・・・ 公式テキスト Chapter9-3

リース資産・リース負債の計上額は $1,200×5.335 = $6,402であるから、初年度の利息は $6,402×10% ≒ $640

# Lease

## 9-5

20X0年12月31日現在、XYZ社が認識すべきリース負債の金額はいくらか。

(1) $5,654

(2) $5,842

(3) $6,175

(4) $6,402

(5) $8,400

### 解答　(2)

解説 ⋯⋯⋯⋯⋯⋯⋯⋯⋯⋯⋯⋯⋯⋯⋯⋯⋯⋯⋯⋯⋯ 公式テキスト Chapter9-3

初年度に減額するリース負債の金額は $1,200 − $640 = $560であるから、期末のリース負債は $6,402 − $560 = $5,842

## 9-6

20X0年12月31日に終了する年度に XYZ 社が認識すべき減価償却費の金額はいくらか。

(1) $0

(2) $618

(3) $640

(4) $771

(5) $800

### 解答　(5)

解説 ⋯⋯⋯⋯⋯⋯⋯⋯⋯⋯⋯⋯⋯⋯⋯⋯⋯⋯⋯⋯⋯ 公式テキスト Chapter9-3

$6,402 ÷ 8年 ≒ $800

解答編

# CHAPTER 10

## Financial Assets

Bookkeeping & Accounting Test for International Communication

# BATIC
Bookkeeper & Accountant Level

**Financial Assets**

### 10-1

ジョーンズ社は20X5年3月1日に£100,000の資本証券を購入した。ジョーンズは証券を公正価値で測定する証券に分類し、その後の公正価値の変動をその他の包括利益で表示する選択を行った。

20X5年10月1日、ジョーンズは£4,000の現金配当を受け取った。20X5年12月31日、証券の公正価値は£105,000であった。

ジョーンズは20X5年12月31日に終了する年度のその他の包括利益にいくら含めるべきか。

(1) £0

(2) £1,000

(3) £4,000

(4) £5,000

(5) £9,000

**解答　(4)**

**解説** ································································ 公式テキスト Chapter10-2

公正価値の上昇分£5,000のみをその他の包括利益に含め、現金配当の£4,000は純損益（profit or loss）に含める。

## Financial Assets

問題2および3は以下に基づく。

20X5年1月1日に、パイナップル社は現金 $10,000 で資本性金融商品を購入し、その他の包括利益を通じた公正価値で測定する商品として指定した。

金融商品の公正価値は以下のようになっている。

| | |
|---|---|
| 20X5年12月31日 | $ 9,000 |
| 20X6年12月31日 | 12,000 |

### 10-2

パイナップル社は 20X6年12月31日に終了する年度にその他の包括利益をいくら認識すべきか。

(1) $0
(2) 借方 $2,000
(3) 貸方 $2,000
(4) 借方 $3,000
(5) 貸方 $3,000

### 解答　(5)

解説 ································································· 公式テキスト Chapter10-2

> 20X5年の仕訳：
> Dr Other comprehensive income　　1,000
> 　　Cr Financial asset　　　　　　　　　　1,000
> 20X6年の仕訳：
> Dr Financial asset　　3,000
> 　　Cr Other comprehensive income　　　3,000

Chapter 10

173

# Financial Assets

## 10-3

パイナップル社は20X7年1月1日に資本性金融商品を$13,000で売却した。20X7年1月1日に行うべき仕訳は以下のどれか。

(1) （借方）現金 13,000
   　　（貸方）金融資産 10,000
   　　　　　　金融資産売却益 3,000

(2) （借方）現金 13,000
   　　（貸方）金融資産 12,000
   　　　　　　金融資産売却益 1,000

(3) （借方）現金 13,000
   　　（貸方）金融資産 10,000
   　　　　　　その他の包括利益 3,000

(4) （借方）現金 13,000
   　　（貸方）金融資産 12,000
   　　　　　　その他の包括利益 1,000

(5) （借方）現金 13,000
   　　　　　　その他の包括利益 2,000
   　　（貸方）金融資産 12,000
   　　　　　　金融資産売却益 3,000

## 解答 （4）

**解説** ‥‥‥‥‥‥‥‥‥‥‥‥‥‥‥‥‥‥‥‥‥‥‥‥ 公式テキスト Chapter10-2

売却目的保有でない資本性金融商品は、FVOCI測定と指定した場合、評価差額はその他の包括利益（OCI）に計上される。OCIに計上された金額はリサイクリングしない、すなわち売却時に売却損益は発生しない。なお、資本内で振替を行うことはできる。

## Financial Assets

### 10-4

トッド社は 20X5 年 12 月 31 日に€ 5,000,000 の負債証券を購入した。当該証券はその他の包括利益を通じて公正価値を測定する資産に分類された。トッドは購入時に信用毀損はないと確定した。

次の情報は 20X5 年 12 月 31 日の予想信用損失に関するものである。

| | |
|---|---|
| 12 か月の予想信用損失 | € 300,000 |
| 全期間の予想信用損失 | € 500,000 |

トッド社が 20X5 年 12 月 31 日に行うべき次の仕訳を完成させよ。

| | | | |
|---|---|---|---|
| （借方）金融資産 ― FVOCI | [          ] | | |
| 減損損失（純損益） | [          ] | | |
| （貸方）現金 | | [          ] | |
| その他の包括利益 | | [          ] | |

**解答**

| | | |
|---|---|---|
| Dr Financial asset ― FVOCI | [5,000,000] | |
| Impairment loss（profit or loss） | [ 300,000] | |
| Cr Cash | | [5,000,000] |
| Other comprehensive income | | [ 300,000] |

**解説** ⋯⋯⋯⋯⋯⋯⋯⋯⋯⋯⋯⋯⋯⋯⋯⋯ 公式テキスト Chapter10-3

FVOCI 測定の金融資産の場合、減損損失を当期の純損益に計上するが、相手勘定は OCI（その他の包括利益）となり、当該資産の簿価を直接減額しない。減損損失の金額は当初より信用毀損がない場合、12 か月の予想信用損失となる。

# Financial Assets

## 10-5

スミス社は売掛金£40,000をファクターに償還請求権なしで売却した。売却にあたって、スミスは売掛金のキャッシュ・フローを受け取る契約上の権利を譲渡した。ファクターのサービス料は3%である。スミスは売掛金の売却損をいくら記録すべきか。

(1) £0

(2) £ 1,200

(3) £38,800

(4) £40,000

(5) 上記のいずれでもない

**解答　(2)**

**解説** ……………………………………………………… 公式テキスト Chapter10-4

仕訳は次のとおり。

Dr Cash　　　　　　　　　　　　　　 38,800

　　Loss on sale of accounts receivable　 1,200　←£40,000×3%

　　　Cr Accounts receivable　　　　　　　 40,000

解答編

**CHAPTER 11**

# Financial Liabilities

Bookkeeping & Accounting Test for International Communication

# BATIC
Bookkeeper & Accountant Level

# Financial Liabilities

## 11-1

ペガサス社は、20X0年9月1日に、額面価額 $1,000,000、利率6%、発行日付が20X0年7月1日で満期までの期間が10年の一括償還社債を発行した。社債は、実効利回りが8%となる価額で発行され、その結果、$864,000に経過利息を足した額を受け取った。利息の支払いは、1月1日と7月1日の年2回である。ペガサスは社債を純損益を通じて公正価値で測定する社債に指定しなかった。20X0年12月31日現在の財政状態計算書において、ペガサス社はいくらの未払利息を計上すべきか。

(1) $20,000

(2) $30,000

(3) $34,560

(4) $40,000

(5) 上記のいずれでもない

**解答　(2)**

**解説** ⋯⋯⋯⋯⋯⋯⋯⋯⋯⋯⋯⋯⋯⋯⋯⋯⋯⋯⋯⋯ 公式テキスト Chapter11-2

本問は社債を割引発行した場合である。20X0年9月1日の社債発行時の経過利息は額面価額 $1,000,000 × 表面金利6% × 経過期間 2/12 ＝ $10,000 となり、Interest payable（未払利息）として計上される。従って、社債発行時の仕訳は次のようになる。

| Dr | Cash | 874,000 | |
|---|---|---|---|
| | Cr Bonds payable | | 864,000 |
| | Interest payable | | 10,000 |

次に、20X0年9月1日から12月31日までの未払利息の計算は、額面価額 $1,000,000 × 表面金利6% × 対象期間 4/12 ＝ $20,000 として算定される。この未払利息の計上のための仕訳は次の通りとなる。

| Dr | Interest expense | 20,000 | |
|---|---|---|---|
| | Cr Interest payable | | 20,000 |

従って、設問の解答となる財政状態計算書に計上すべき未払利息額は $10,000 + $20,000 = $30,000となる。

なお、20X0年の Discount on bonds payable の償却金額は、次のように算定される。

額面価額 $1,000,000 × 表面金利 6% × 対象期間 6/12 = $30,000
発行価額 $864,000 × 実効金利 8% × 対象期間 6/12 = $34,560
$34,560 − $30,000 = ディスカウント償却額 $4,560

仕訳は次の通りである。

| Dr | Interest expense | 4,560 | |
|---|---|---|---|
| | Cr Bonds payable | | 4,560 |

## Financial Liabilities

### 11-2

20X1年1月1日に、スチュアート社は額面価額€500,000、年率8%、満期日が20X9年1月1日の社債を額面発行した。利息の支払いは7月1日と1月1日の年2回である。スチュアートは純損益を通じて公正価値で測定する社債として指定しなかった。以下の取引を記帳するために必要な仕訳をせよ。

(a) 社債の発行
(b) 20X1年7月1日の利息の支払い
(c) 20X2年3月31日時点で記帳すべき経過利息

解答　(a) Dr Cash　　　　　　　　500,000
　　　　　　 Cr Bonds payable　　　　　　　500,000

　　　 (b) Dr Interest expense　　20,000
　　　　　　 Cr Cash　　　　　　　　　　　20,000

　　　 (c) Dr Interest expense　　10,000
　　　　　　 Cr Interest payable　　　　　　10,000

解説 ·········································· 公式テキスト Chapter11-2

(b) €500,000×8%×6/12 = €20,000

(c) €500,000×8%×3/12 = €10,000

180

## Financial Liabilities

### 11-3

BBB 社は次の普通社債を発行した。

| | |
|---|---|
| 発行日 | 20X1 年 1 月 1 日 |
| 満期日 | 20X4 年 12 月 31 日 |
| 額面価額 | €80,000 |
| 表面金利 | 4% |
| 実効金利 | 5% |
| 利息の支払い | 年に一回 12 月 31 日 |

BBB は純損益を通じて公正価値で測定する社債として指定しなかった。

計算にあたっては、次の現在価値情報を使用せよ。

割引率 5% での 4 年間の 1 の期末年金の現在価値　　3.5459

割引率 5% での 4 年後の 1 の現在価値　　　　　　　0.8227

次の金額を計算せよ。必要があれば、各金額の小数点以下を四捨五入せよ。

(1) 発行価額

(2) 20X1 年 1 月 1 日現在の社債のディスカウント

(3) 20X1 年 12 月 31 日に終了する年度の支払利息

(4) 20X1 年 12 月 31 日現在の社債のディスカウント

# Financial Liabilities

**解答**　(1) € 77,163

　　　　(2) €　2,837

　　　　(3) €　3,858

　　　　(4) €　2,179

**解説** ················································· 公式テキスト Chapter11-2

(1) 額面価額の現在価値は€80,000 × 0.8227 = €65,816

　　利息の総支払額の現在価値は€80,000×4%×3.5459 = €11,346.88 ≒ €11,347

　　したがって発行価額は€65,816 + €11,347 = €77,163

(2) €80,000 − €77,163 = €2,837

(3) €77,163 × 5% ≒ €3,858

(4) ディスカウントの償却額　€77,163 × 5% − €3,200 = €658

　　したがってディスカウントの残高は€2,837 − €658 = €2,179

解答編

**CHAPTER 12**

# Provisions, Contingent Liabilities and Contingent Assets

Bookkeeping & Accounting Test for International Communication

# BATIC
Bookkeeper & Accountant Level

# Provisions, Contingent Liabilities and Contingent Assets

**問題1および2は以下に基づく。**

次の状況は奈良モーターに関するものである。

a. 奈良は京都㈱の特許の不正使用による被害に対して訴訟を起こした。奈良はおそらく勝訴し、¥70,000,000を得るであろう。

b. 住民が奈良の工場から排出されるガスによる健康被害を訴えた。弁護士の予測によると、奈良はおそらく裁判に負け、¥100,000,000から¥300,000,000の間の金額を支払うことになるであろう。支払い金額の最善の見積りは¥250,000,000である。

c. ある顧客が製品の欠陥によるけがについて奈良を訴えた。弁護士は奈良が敗訴する可能性は高くないが、仮に敗訴した場合は¥600,000,000支払うことになるだろうと述べた。

d. 元従業員がある特許の開発に対して¥100,000,000の報奨を受ける権利があると主張している。弁護士の判断は、特許の重要な部分は他の同僚によって開発されたものであるから、たとえ訴訟を起こしても会社側が敗訴することはないであろうというものである。

## 12-1

奈良は引当金としていくら認識しなくてはならないか。

(1) ¥180,000,000

(2) ¥250,000,000

(3) ¥600,000,000

(4) ¥800,000,000

(5) ¥900,000,000

## Provisions, Contingent Liabilities and Contingent Assets

### 解答　(2)

解説 ……………………………………………………… 公式テキスト Chapter12-2

| | | |
|---|---|---|
| (a) | ¥0 | 偶発資産は認識しない。Probable（可能性が大きい）な場合のみ注記する。 |
| (b) | ¥250,000,000 | 現在の債務があり、経済的便益が流出する可能性が高いので、最善の見積りについて引当金を認識する。 |
| (c) | ¥0 | 現在の債務はないので、引当金は認識しない。経済的便益が流出する可能性はあるので、偶発負債として開示する。 |
| (d) | ¥0 | 現在の債務はないので、引当金は認識しない。経済的便益が流出する可能性がほとんどないので、偶発負債の開示も行わない。 |

### 12-2

引当金として認識はされないが注記として開示されるのはどれか。

(1) (a)，(b) のみ

(2) (a)，(c) のみ

(3) (a)，(c)，(d) のみ

(4) (b)，(c)，(d) のみ

(5) (c)，(d) のみ

### 解答　(2)

解説……………………………………………………… 公式テキスト Chapter12-2

問題 12-1 の解説を参照。

185

# Provisions, Contingent Liabilities and Contingent Assets

## 12-3

ハン社の取締役会は、同社の事業のうちの一つから撤退することを決定した。そのリストラクチャリングに関して、次のようなコストが発生すると予想している。

(a) その事業で使用していた資産に関する長期リースの解約違約金

(b) その事業の資産を他の事業に移転させるコスト

(c) 他の事業に異動する従業員の再教育コスト

(d) 撤退完了までに発生すると予想される将来の営業損失

(e) 撤退の結果として行う新しいソフトウェアシステムへの投資

(f) 撤退に関する不利な契約の引当金

そのリストラクチャリング計画は引当金の認識要件を満たしている。上のコストのうち、リストラクチャリング引当金に含まれなければならないのはどれか。

(1) (a) および (d) のみ

(2) (a) および (f) のみ

(3) (a), (b) および (e) のみ

(4) (a), (b) および (f) のみ

(5) (a), (c) および (e) のみ

### 解答 （2）

### 解説 ·································· 公式テキスト Chapter12-4

リストラクチャリングから発生する直接的な支出で、リストラクチャリングに必然的に伴い、かつ企業の継続的な活動に関連しない支出だけがリストラクチャリング引当金に含まれる。将来の事業遂行に関連するコストは含まれない。

解答編

# CHAPTER 13

## Equity

Bookkeeping & Accounting Test for International Communication

# BATIC
Bookkeeper & Accountant Level

# Equity

## 13-1

20X0年4月1日においてダート社の普通株式は50,000株流通していた。6月15日ダート社は2対1の株式分割をおこなった。その時点で株式は1株あたり$70の市場価格であった。11月30日には1株あたり$1の現金配当を宣言した。これ以外の取引はなかった。20X0年12月31日においてダート社の未払配当金はいくらか。

(1) $0
(2) $100,000
(3) $150,000
(4) $225,000
(5) 上記のいずれでもない

### 解答　(2)

**解説** ················································· 公式テキスト Chapter13-3

株式分割の仕訳は必要ないが、6月15日の株式分割により株式数は100,000株へと増加しているので、20X0年12月31日における未払配当金は$100,000（100,000株×$1）となる。

# Equity

### 13-2

20X0年7月1日、クレー社は事業を開始し、普通株式40,000株を1株あたり$10で発行し、全額資本金とした。20X2年10月1日、クレー社は5,000株を$200,000で買い戻し、そのうち3,000株を$135,000で20X2年12月31日に売却した。

自己株式の消却時における仕訳を正しく示しているのはどれか。

(1)（借方）現金                              135,000

　　　（貸方）資本剰余金—自己株式                          135,000

(2)（借方）現金                              135,000

　　　（貸方）自己株式                                      120,000

　　　　　　　資本金                                        15,000

(3)（借方）現金                              135,000

　　　（貸方）自己株式                                      135,000

(4)（借方）現金                              135,000

　　　（貸方）自己株式                                      120,000

　　　　　　　資本剰余金—自己株式                          15,000

(5) 仕訳の必要はない。

# Equity

## 解答　(4)

**解説** ………………………………………………… 公式テキスト Chapter13-4

買戻し時の仕訳は以下の通り。

Dr Treasury Shares 200,000
　Cr Cash 200,000

買戻し時に計上した自己株式を取り崩し、処分差益を Share premium-treasury に計上する。

一株当たりの買戻し価格 ：$40（$200,000÷5,000株 ＝ $40）
一株当たりの売却価格 ：$45（$135,000÷3,000株 ＝ $45）
処分差益 ：$15,000（$3,000×（$45 － $40）＝ $15,000）

# Equity

## 13-3

20X0年12月31日、ABC社は20X2年12月31日に満期日を迎える転換社債を発行し、$70,000を得た。発行日における社債の負債部分の公正価値は$50,000、資本部分の公正価値は$24,000であった。ABC社は20X0年12月31日現在の貸借対照表でどのように転換社債を表示すべきか。

| | 負債 | 資本 |
|---|---|---|
| (1) | $0 | $70,000 |
| (2) | $50,000 | $0 |
| (3) | $50,000 | $20,000 |
| (4) | $50,000 | $24,000 |
| (5) | $70,000 | $0 |

**解答　(3)**

**解説** ················································· 公式テキスト Chapter13-5

まず負債部分の金額を算定し、金融商品全体の公正価値から負債部分の金額を控除した残額が資本となる。

解答編

# CHAPTER 14

## Revenue Recognition

Bookkeeping & Accounting Test for International Communication

# BATIC

Bookkeeper & Accountant Level

## Revenue Recognition

### 14-1

IFRS 15において、企業が顧客との契約を会計処理する場合に満たすべき要件として最も適切なものは次のうちどれか？

(1) その契約は、企業の将来キャッシュ・フローの金額に影響を与えることが見込まれない。

(2) 企業は、履行の結果として移転される財またはサービスの支配を得る可能性が高い。

(3) 企業は契約を文書で承認したが、義務の履行を確約していない。

(4) 企業は、移転される財またはサービスに関する各当事者の権利を識別できる。

(5) 企業は、移転される財またはサービスの支払い条件を未決定のままにしている。

**解答　(4)**

解説……………………………………………………………… 公式テキスト Chapter14-2

(1) は、経済的実質の要件を満たしていない。(2) については、移転される財またはサービスの支配を得るのは顧客になる。(3) では、企業は義務の履行を確約（commit）していなければならない。(5) では、支払い条件を識別できなければならない。

### 14-2

20X4年1月1日、ヴェンゲル社は、顧客の事務所を毎週清掃する2年契約を締結した。同日、ヴェンゲル社は、各週の清掃サービスは別個のものであると評価した。毎週の清掃サービスは実質的に同じ一連の別個のサービスであり、顧客への移転パターンが同じである。顧客は年額€48,000の支払いを約束した。これは、20X4年1月1日時点における清掃サービスの独立販売価格だった。

20X4年12月31日に契約が変更され、20X5年のサービス料が€45,000に減額された。同日、契約が2年延長され、顧客は延長された2年間の期首ごとに€42,000

を支払うことで合意した。提供されるべき残りのサービスは別個のものである。20X5年1月1日時点の清掃サービスの独立販売価格は€45,000だった。

ヴェンゲル社は、この契約からの収益として残りの3年間にわたって毎年いくら認識すべきか。

(1) €42,000
(2) €43,000
(3) €45,000
(4) €46,500
(5) €48,000

## 解答 (2)

**解説** ································································· 公式テキスト Chapter14-3

毎週の清掃サービスは実質的に同じ一連の別個のサービスであり、また顧客への移転パターンが同じなので、この清掃サービスを単一の履行義務として処理する。契約変更後に支払われるべき残りの金額である€129,000（€45,000×1年＋€42,000×2年）は、延長された2年間を加えた20X5年から3年間の契約の独立販売価格の適切な見積額、€135,000（€45,000×3年）を反映していない。したがって、契約の変更の会計処理の要求事項に従って、当初の契約の終了、および新しい契約の創出であるかのように契約の変更を処理する。

€129,000（€45,000×1年＋€42,000×2年）÷3年＝€43,000

# Revenue Recognition

**問題 3 および 4 は以下に基づく。**

20X0 年 1 月 1 日、スカイ建設社は、顧客の土地に顧客のためのショッピングセンター
を建設する長期請負工事契約を結んだ。この契約における約束された対価は $4,200,000
である。スカイ社は、契約における財とサービスの束を、一定期間にわたり充足さ
れる単一の履行義務として会計処理する。履行義務の完全な充足に向けた進捗度を
測定するため、スカイ社は発生した原価を基礎としたインプット法を使用する。以
下は 20X0 年 12 月 31 日で終了する会計年度のデータである。

| | |
|---|---|
| 累積発生工事原価 | $1,000,000 |
| 見積工事契約総原価 | 4,000,000 |
| 請求金額 | 1,500,000 |
| 現金回収額 | 1,100,000 |

## 14-3

20X0 年にスカイ社が認識すべき収益はいくらか。

(1) $1,050,000

(2) $1,100,000

(3) $1,400,000

(4) $1,500,000

(5) $3,200,000

**解答　(1)**

**解説** ................................................................ 公式テキスト Chapter14-6

1,000,000 ÷ 4,000,000 = 25%

工事契約収益：$4,200,000 × 25% = $1,050,000

Revenue Recognition

## 14-4

20X0年にスカイ社が認識すべき売上総利益はいくらか。

(1) $ 50,000

(2) $100,000

(3) $200,000

(4) $400,000

(5) $500,000

### 解答 （1）

**解説** ································································· 公式テキスト Chapter14-6

$1,050,000（当期工事契約収益）－ $1,000,000（当期工事契約原価）＝ $50,000

## 14-5

ミュラー社は、ベイル社のデータセンターを6年間管理する契約を結んだ。この契約を獲得するために、ミュラー社には€ 12,000の販売手数料が発生した。ミュラー社は、この販売手数料について、管理サービスに係る将来の報酬から回収可能であると見込んでいる。サービス履行前には、ベイル社のシステムと接続するための技術プラットフォームを構築している。技術プラットフォームの構築で発生したコストは次のとおりである。

| | |
|---|---|
| ハードウェア | €150,000 |
| ソフトウェア | 100,000 |
| データセンターの移設とテスト | 80,000 |

上記表中のコストは契約を履行するための活動に関するものであるが、ベイル社に財またはサービスを移転するものではない。ミュラー社は、データセンターの移設とテストのためのコストは回収可能ではないと見込んでいる。

## Revenue Recognition

ミュラー社がIFRS 15に従って資産として認識すべき契約獲得の増分コストおよび契約履行のためのコストの金額はいくらか。

| | 契約獲得の増分コスト | 契約履行のためのコスト |
|---|---|---|
| (1) | € 0 | € 0 |
| (2) | € 0 | € 80,000 |
| (3) | € 12,000 | € 0 |
| (4) | € 12,000 | € 100,000 |
| (5) | € 12,000 | € 250,000 |

### 解答 （3）

**解説** ……………………………………………………… 公式テキスト Chapter14-7

> 販売手数料は回収が見込まれるので、資産として認識する。ハードウェアは、IAS 16に従って有形固定資産として認識する。ソフトウェアは、IAS 38に従って無形資産として認識する。データセンターの移設とテストのためのコストは、回収が見込まれないので資産として認識しない。

**Revenue Recognition**

## 14-6

シティ社は、委託販売の商品£40,000をコスモス社に送った。コスモス社は、受け取った商品の半分を£36,000で販売し、シティ社に通知した。コスモス社の手数料は顧客への販売価格の20%である。シティ社は本人であり、顧客に移転される前の商品を支配している。コスモス社は代理人であり、シティ社の代わりに商品を販売する。

コスモス社がこの販売からの収益として認識すべき金額はいくらか。

(1) £ 7,200
(2) £ 8,000
(3) £18,000
(4) £20,000
(5) £36,000

**解答 (1)**

**解説** ·········································· 公式テキスト Chapter14-9

£36,000 × 20% = £7,200
代理人は、本人のために回収した金額は収益として認識しない。手数料の額が収益になる。

解答編

# CHAPTER 15

## Employee Benefits

Bookkeeping & Accounting Test for International Communication

# BATIC
Bookkeeper & Accountant Level

**Employee Benefits**

### 15-1

以下はある会社の確定給付型年金制度に関するものである。12月31日が年度末となっている。

| | |
|---|---:|
| 20X6年12月31日の確定給付債務の現在価値 | € 56,000 |
| 20X6年12月31日の制度資産の公正価値 | 62,000 |
| 20X6年12月31日のアセット・シーリング | 4,000 |

確定給付負債または資産の金額を算出しなさい。

**解答　Asset, € 4,000**

**解説** ·········································· 公式テキスト Chapter15-4

積立超過額：€ 6,000（€ 62,000 − € 56,000 ＝ € 6,000）
確定給付資産は、積立超過額とアセット・シーリングのいずれか低い方で認識する。よって、確定給付資産は€ 4,000となる。

# Employee Benefits

**問題2から5は以下に基づく。**

次の情報はABC社の確定給付型年金制度に関するものである。税金は無視しなさい。

| | |
|---|---:|
| 20X8年1月1日： | |
| 確定給付制度債務の現在価値 | |
| （過去勤務費用を含む） | $2,500,000 |
| 制度資産の公正価値 | 2,340,000 |
| 過去勤務費用 * | 620,000 |
| | |
| 20X8年中： | |
| 当期勤務費用 | $630,000 |
| 制度資産に係る収益 | 190,000 |
| 拠出額 | 50,000 |
| 給付額 | 30,000 |
| | |
| 20X8年12月31日： | |
| 確定給付制度債務の現在価値 | |
| （数理計算上の損失を含む） | $3,410,000 |
| 制度資産の公正価値 | 2,550,000 |
| 数理計算上の損失 ** | 210,000 |
| | |
| 割引率：4% | |

\* 過去勤務費用は20X8年1月1日末に年金制度が改定されたことにより生じたものである。

\*\*数理計算上の損失は20X8年末に将来の従業員の離職に関する仮定が改定されたことにより生じたものである。

20X7年12月31日にアセット・シーリングの影響はなかった。

# Employee Benefits

## 15-2

20X8年12月31日現在の確定給付負債／資産は、

(1) $3,410,000の負債

(2) $1,370,000の負債

(3) $ 860,000の負債

(4) $ 210,000の資産

(5) $2,550,000の資産

### 解答　(3)

**解説** ·················································· 公式テキスト Chapter15-4

$3,410,000 − $2,550,000 = $860,000

## 15-3

20X8年12月31日に終了する年度の利息純額は、

(1) $　6,400

(2) $ 93,600

(3) $100,000

(4) $102,000

(5) $193,600

### 解答　(1)

**解説** ·················································· 公式テキスト Chapter15-4

期首の確定給付負債の純額 × 割引率＝（$2,500,000 − $2,340,000）×4%

= $6,400

# Employee Benefits

## 15-4

20X8年12月31日に終了する年度の純損益で認識する確定給付費用は、

(1) $ 636,400

(2) $ 820,000

(3) $1,250,000

(4) $1,256,400

(5) $1,440,000

### 解答　(4)

**解説** ···················································· 公式テキスト Chapter15-4

過去勤務費用（past service cost）、当期勤務費用（current service cost）、
利息純額を純損益に認識する。

$620,000 + $630,000 + $6,400 = $1,256,400

## 15-5

20X8年12月31日に終了する年度の、その他の包括利益で認識する確定給付費用は、

(1) $ 20,000

(2) $113,600

(3) $210,000

(4) $306,400

(5) $400,000

### 解答　(2)

**解説** ···················································· 公式テキスト Chapter15-4

数理計算上の損失（actuarial loss）と、利息純額に含まれる金額を除いた制
度資産に係る収益（return on plan assets）をその他の包括利益に認識する。

$210,000 − （$190,000 − $2,340,000×4%） = $113,600

## Employee Benefits

### 15-6

20X5年1月1日、ブラック社は、同社の普通株式 10,000 株を 1 株あたり $25 で購入できるストック・オプションを従業員に与えた。当日の市場価格は同じ $25 であり、ストック・オプションの公正価値は $6 であった。従業員は要求されている勤務終了後 20X8 年 1 月 1 日からオプションを行使できる。20X5 年 12 月 31 日、株価及びストックオプションの公正価値は、それぞれ $23 および $2.5 であった。

20X5年、ブラック社が認識すべき報酬費用はいくらか。

(1) $0

(2) $ 20,000

(3) $ 25,000

(4) $ 60,000

(5) $140,000

**解答　(2)**

**解説** ················································· 公式テキスト Chapter15-5

$6 × 10,000 株 /3 年 = $20,000

## Employee Benefits

### 15-7

ある企業の従業員は20X5年1月1日に次のような2種類のストック・オプションを与えられた。

|  | オプション数 | オプションの<br>公正価値 |
|---|---|---|
| プラン A | 1,000 | $10 |
| プラン B | 1,000 | $12 |

プラン A のストック・オプションは20X6年1月1日から行使可能である。このオプションは20X4年の従業員の成績に対する報酬として与えられる。

プラン B のストック・オプションは従業員が必要な勤務を完了する20X8年1月1日から行使可能である。

企業が20X5年に認識すべき報酬費用はいくらになるか。

(1) $0

(2) $ 4,000

(3) $10,000

(4) $14,000

(5) $22,000

## 解答 (4)

**解説** ………………………………………………………… 公式テキスト Chapter15-5

Plan A に関しては権利が確定した報酬なので、付与日に全額認識する。

$10×1,000株 = $10,000

Plan B に関しては一定期間にわたるサービスが完了するまで権利が確定しない報酬なので、サービス提供期間に渡って按分する。

$12×1,000株 ÷ 3年 = $4,000

従って認識すべき報酬費用の総額は、

$10,000 + $4,000 = $14,000

解答編

**CHAPTER 16**

# Income Taxes

Bookkeeping & Accounting Test for International Communication

# BATIC
Bookkeeper & Accountant Level

**Income Taxes**

<u>問題1および2は以下に基づく。</u>

AAA社は20X0年1月1日に事業を開始し、20X0年の会計上の収益は$200,000、税務上の収益は$170,000であった。また、AAA社は会計上税務上ともに$100,000の費用があった。税率は30%である。

**16-1**

AAA社の20X0年の未払法人税の金額は以下のうちどれか。

(1) $ 9,000
(2) $21,000
(3) $30,000
(4) $51,000
(5) 上記のいずれでもない

**解答　(2)**

**解説** ································································ 公式テキスト Chapter16-3

$($170,000 − 100,000$) \times 30\% = $21,000$

Income Taxes

## 16-2

20X0年の財政状態計算書において、AAA社の繰延税金負債は以下のうちどれか。

(1) $ 9,000

(2) $21,000

(3) $30,000

(4) $39,000

(5) 上記のいずれでもない

解答　(1)

**解説** ……………………………………………… 公式テキスト Chapter16-4

会計上の利益 $100,000（= $200,000 − 100,000)、税務上の利益 $70,000（=
$170,000 − 100,000)。[税引前利益 $100,000 − 課税所得 $70,000] 分は、当期に
は課税されないが、将来課税されるので繰延税金負債として認識される。
Deferred tax liability = Future taxable amount × Enacted tax rate となり
$30,000 × 30% = $9,000。

Chapter 16

211

# Income Taxes

## 16-3

フラム社は、20X3年12月31日に終了にする会計年度に、£77,000の製品保証費を会計上の利益に含めて報告した。税務報告目的上は、£20,000が20X3年に損金計上できるが、残りは20X4年に損金計上できる予想である。法定税率は20X3年以降30%である。

20X3年12月31日現在の財政状態計算書において、フラム社は繰延税金資産をいくら流動あるいは非流動として報告すべきか。

|     | 流動 | 非流動 |
| --- | --- | --- |
| (1) | – | £ 6,000 |
| (2) | – | £17,100 |
| (3) | – | £23,100 |
| (4) | £ 6,000 | £17,100 |
| (5) | £17,100 | – |

**解答　(2)**

**解説** ················································· 公式テキスト Chapter16-4

繰延税金資産＝（£77,000 － £20,000）×30% ＝£17,100
なお、繰延税金資産・負債はすべて非流動に分類しなければならない。

Income Taxes

<u>問題 4 から 6 は以下に基づく。</u>

アプリコット社は、米国の会社である。20X0年1月1日に設立され、20X0年に $39,000 の税引前利益を計上した。下記の情報は20X0年の所得税に関するものである。

● 税引前利益には、地方債からの利息 $2,300、罰金の支払い $1,000 が含まれており、税務上、どちらも永久に加減算されない。
● また、税引前利益には製品保証費 $4,400 が含まれており、そのうち $1,000 のみが税務上 20X0年に減算できる。
● アプリコット社は税務上と会計上で異なる減価償却方法を使用している。下記の表は、各年度末の減価償却資産の税務上及び帳簿上の価額を示している。

|  | 20X0 | 20X1 | 20X2 | 20X3 |
|---|---|---|---|---|
| 税務上 | $15,000 | $ 7,000 | $2,000 | $0 |
| 帳簿上 | 20,000 | 10,000 | 0 | 0 |

● 法定税率は 20X0年及びそれ以降 30% である。

該当があれば、繰延税金資産・負債は相殺し、繰延税金資産は全額回収可能と仮定せよ。

213

## Income Taxes

### 16-4

20X0年12月31日現在の財政状態計算書において、未払法人税として報告すべき金額を計算せよ。

**解答** $10,830

**解説** ·········································· 公式テキスト Chapter16-1,4

$39,000 − $2,300 + $1,000 + $3,400 − $5,000 = $36,100

$36,100 × 30% = $10,830

### 16-5

20X0年の財務諸表において、繰延税金費用を記録するための仕訳をせよ。

**解答**　Dr Income tax expense — deferred　480
　　　　　　Cr Deferred tax liabilities　　　　　480

**解説** ·········································· 公式テキスト Chapter16-1,4

繰延税金資産・負債は相殺するので、($5,000 − $3,400) × 30% = $480の繰延税金負債及び繰延税金費用を計上することになる。

### 16-6

20X0年12月31日に終了する年度の損益計算書において、当期利益として報告する金額を計算せよ。

**解答** $27,690

**解説** ·········································· 公式テキスト Chapter16-1,4

$39,000 − ($10,830 + $480) = $27,690

## Income Taxes

### 16-7

ワンセント社は $60,000 の将来減算一時差異による繰延税金資産を記録するため、以下の仕訳を行った。法定税率は 25% であった。

（借方）繰延税金資産　　　　　　　15,000
　　（貸方）繰延税金費用　　　　　　　15,000

その後、ワンセント社は繰延税金資産の 60% のみ回収可能であると測定した。ワンセントは、繰延税金資産の 60% のみ回収可能であると測定した際に、以下のどの仕訳を行うべきか。

(1)（借方）当期税金費用　　　　　　　6,000
　　（貸方）未払法人税　　　　　　　　　　6,000
(2)（借方）繰延税金費用　　　　　　　6,000
　　（貸方）繰延税金資産控除引当金　　　　6,000
(3)（借方）繰延税金費用　　　　　　　6,000
　　（貸方）繰延税金資産　　　　　　　　　6,000
(4)（借方）繰延税金費用　　　　　　　9,000
　　（貸方）繰延税金資産　　　　　　　　　9,000
(5) 仕訳は必要ない。

### 解答　(3)

解説 ……………………………………………………… 公式テキスト Chapter16-4

> 繰延税金資産は回収可能性がある場合のみ財務諸表に計上を認められる。したがって、回収可能性がない 40％分（$15,000×40%=$6,000）を減額する仕訳を行う。その際、評価性引当金を用いず直接減額しなければならない。

Chapter 16

215

解答編

# CHAPTER 17

## Statement of Cash Flows

Bookkeeping & Accounting Test for International Communication

# BATIC

Bookkeeper & Accountant Level

## Statement of Cash Flows

### 17-1

固定資産の売却による現金の受領は、キャッシュ・フロー計算書のどの区分に報告されるべきか。

(1) 財務活動

(2) 営業活動

(3) 投資活動

(4) 販売活動

(5) 上記のいずれでもない

**解答　(3)**

**解説** ………………………………………………………… 公式テキスト Chapter17-2

投資活動には、有形・無形固定資産やその他の長期保有資産の変動に伴う
キャッシュ・フロー取引が含まれる。

Statement of Cash Flows

## 17-2

グリーン社は20X0年12月31日に終了する会計年度の損益計算書で€115,000の当期純利益を計上した。以下が20X0年度の当期純利益算出のための情報である。

| | |
|---|---|
| 減価償却費 | € 8,500 |
| 機器売却損 | 8,230 |
| パイン社への持分法による投資利益 | 12,500 |

20X0年におけるグリーン社の営業活動によるキャッシュ・フローはいくらか。

(1) €110,770

(2) €119,230

(3) €121,130

(4) €127,430

(5) €127,770

### 解答 （2）

**解説** ‥‥‥‥‥‥‥‥‥‥‥‥‥‥‥‥‥‥‥‥‥‥‥ 公式テキスト Chapter17-2

たとえば減価償却費では、資産を購入した時点ではキャッシュが出ていくが、その後はキャッシュを伴わない減価償却費となって利益を減少させる。損益計算書では費用に含まれているので、キャッシュ・フロー計算書では下記のようにプラス調整して、この費用を取り消さなければならない。設問の例はすべて非資金損益項目（Non-cash items）なので、キャッシュの流入出を伴わないため、調整が必要となる。

| | |
|---|---|
| 当期純利益 | €115,000 |
| 減価償却費 | 8,500 |
| 機器売却損 | 8,230 |
| パイン社への持分法による投資利益 | (12,500) |
| | €119,230 |

## Statement of Cash Flows

**問題3から5は以下に基づく。**

下記の情報は20X2年12月31日のABC社のキャッシュ・フロー計算書を間接法のもとで作成するにあたり使用される情報である。

①20X2年1月2日にABCは取得原価$600,000、簿価$240,000の設備を$260,000の現金払いで売却した。

②ABCは20X2年11月20日に$2,000,000の支払手形を発行して新しい設備を購入した。

　尚、支払手形の支払期日は20X3年3月20日である。

③ABCは20X2年12月31日に償却原価で測定される有価証券の減損損失を$300,000計上した。

④ABCは20X2年に$650,000の長期借入金を一年内返済予定の長期借入金に組替えた。

⑤ABCはFG銀行から20X2年4月15日に$300,000の長期借入を行った。

⑥ABCは20X2年5月20日に$500,000の社債を発行した。

⑦ABCは20X2年の間に、普通株式の発行により$3,400,000の資金調達を行った。

⑧ABCは20X2年の間に$550,000の配当を発表し現金で配当を支払った。

## Statement of Cash Flows

**17-3**

上記の情報をもとに、当期純利益から営業活動によるネット・キャッシュ・フローへの調整を行うための修正額を求めよ。

(1) $ (100,000)

(2) $  50,000

(3) $ 100,000

(4) $ 280,000

(5) $ 350,000

### 解答　(4)

**解説** ·················································· 公式テキスト Chapter17-3

営業活動に関するキャッシュ・フローを伴わない取引の調整仕訳

①設備売却（固定資産売却益）のキャッシュ・フロー調整仕訳

| | | |
|---|---|---|
| Dr  Equipment | 600,000 | |
| 　Decrease CF for gain on sale of equipment | 20,000 | |
| 　Cr Cash inflow from sale of equipment | | 260,000 |
| 　　Accumulated depreciation | | 360,000 |

③有価証券減損損失の戻し仕訳

| | | |
|---|---|---|
| Dr  Investment | 300,000 | |
| 　Cr Increase CF for impairment loss | | 300,000 |

営業活動に関する Cash flows を伴わない取引の調整額

$300,000 - $20,000 = $280,000

（※）なお⑧の支払配当金を営業活動に含める場合は $280,000 - $550,000 = $ (270,000) となる。

# Statement of Cash Flows

## 17-4

上記の情報をもとに、投資活動によるネット・キャッシュ・フローの額を求めよ。

(1) $ 240,000

(2) $ 260,000

(3) $ 600,000

(4) $2,260,000

(5) $2,600,000

**解答 (2)**

**解説** ................................................................ 公式テキスト Chapter17-3

投資活動に関する調整仕訳の計上

①設備売却のキャッシュ・フロー調整仕訳

　17-3 ① 参照

②設備購入時の仕訳は、

　Dr Equipment　　　　　　　　　　2,000,000

　　Cr Notes payable　　　　　　　　　　　　　2,000,000

　で Cash が流出していない為、Cash の増減なし。

従って、投資活動に関する Cash inflow は、$260,000 となる。

# Statement of Cash Flows

## 17-5

上記の情報をもとに財務活動によるネット・キャッシュ・フローの額を求めよ。

(1) $ (3,650,000)

(2) $ (3,150,000)

(3) $ 2,050,000

(4) $ 3,650,000

(5) $ 4,750,000

**解答　(4)**

解説 …………………………………………… 公式テキスト Chapter17-3

財務活動に関する調整仕訳の計上

④長期、短期組替えの仕訳

| Dr Long-term debt | 650,000 | |
| Cr Long-term debt within one-year | | 650,000 |

で Cash の増減なし。

⑤長期借入金新規借入のキャッシュ・フロー調整仕訳

| Dr Long-term debt | 300,000 | |
| Cr Cash inflow from long-term debt | | 300,000 |

⑥社債発行のキャッシュ・フロー調整仕訳

| Dr Bonds | 500,000 | |
| Cr Cash inflow from issuing bonds | | 500,000 |

⑦普通株式発行のキャッシュ・フロー調整仕訳

| Dr Ordinary shares | 3,400,000 | |
| Cr Cash inflow from issuing ordinary shares | | 3,400,000 |

# Statement of Cash Flows

⑧配当金支払いのキャッシュ・フロー調整仕訳

Dr Cash outflow for payment of dividends    550,000

    Cr Retained earnings       550,000

従って、財務活動に関する Cash inflow は

$300,000 + $500,000 + $3,400,000 - $550,000 = $3,650,000

となる。

（※）なお⑧の支払配当金を営業活動に含める場合は $4,200,000 となる。

## 17-6

営業活動によるキャッシュ・フローとして分類できないものは、次のうちどの項目か。

(1) 配当の現金支払
(2) サプライヤーに対する代金の現金支払
(3) 商品販売による現金受取
(4) 利息の現金受取
(5) 借入金の現金返済

**解答　(5)**

解説……………………………………………………… 公式テキスト Chapter17-2

借入金の現金返済は Financing activities（財務活動）に分類される。

解答編

**CHAPTER 18**

# Business Combinations /
# Consolidated Statements

Bookkeeping & Accounting Test for International Communication

# BATIC
Bookkeeper & Accountant Level

## Business Combinations / Consolidated Statements

### 18-1

取得企業は取得日に被取得企業の非支配持分をどのように測定すべきか。

(1) 公正価値

(2) 被取得企業の識別可能な純資産の比例持分額

(3) 公正価値か被取得企業の識別可能な純資産の比例持分額

(4) 公正価値か被取得企業の識別可能な純資産の比例持分額のいずれか高い方

(5) 上記のいずれでもない

**解答　(3)**

解説‥‥‥‥‥‥‥‥‥‥‥‥‥‥‥‥‥‥‥‥‥‥‥‥‥ 公式テキスト Chapter18-2

被支配持分は公正価値または純資産の比例持分額のいずれかで測定すること
となっており、どちらも認められている。

### 18-2

次の空欄を埋める適切な番号を選びなさい。

他の企業に投資を行う企業は、投資企業自身が被投資会社 [　　　　　] かどうか
を評価することによって、被投資会社を連結するかどうか決定しなければならない。

(1) に恩恵をもたらしている

(2) を支配している

(3) を規定している

(4) を所有している

(5) を支援している

**解答　(2)**

## Business Combinations / Consolidated Statements

解説⋯⋯⋯⋯⋯⋯⋯⋯⋯⋯⋯⋯⋯⋯⋯⋯⋯⋯⋯ 公式テキスト Chapter18-5

> 連結するかどうかの判定は、Control（支配）があるかどうかで決まる。支
> 配があれば連結し、なければ連結しない。なお、Control は動詞・名詞、両
> 方使う。

### 18-3

20X0年1月1日、ピクシー社はスタイル社の株式の80%を現金 $1,300,000 と引
き換えに取得した。同日、スタイル社の棚卸資産以外の資産および負債は、時価
および簿価共にそれぞれ $1,470,000 と $350,000 であったが、棚卸資産については、
時価 $260,000、簿価 $180,000 であった。非支配持分の公正価値は $280,000 であっ
た。ピクシーはスタイルの非支配持分をスタイルの識別可能な純資産の比例持分
額で測定することを選択した。

上記の情報より 20X0年1月1日現在の連結財政状態計算書に計上すべきのれん
の金額を計算せよ。

解答　$196,000

解説 ⋯⋯⋯⋯⋯⋯⋯⋯⋯⋯⋯⋯⋯⋯⋯⋯⋯⋯⋯ 公式テキスト Chapter18-6

> スタイル社の純資産の公正価値は、$1,470,000（資産）＋ $260,000（棚卸資
> 産（時価））− $350,000（負債）＝ $1,380,000 となる。したがってのれんの金
> 額は、$1,300,000 ＋ $1,380,000 × 20％ − $1,380,000 ＝ $196,000 となる。

## Business Combinations / Consolidated Statements

<u>問題 4 および 5 は以下に基づく。</u>

プライム社は 20X0年初めにサン社の普通株式 70% を取得した。以下は 20X0年におけるプライム社とサン社のデータの一部である。

|  | プライム社 | サン社 |
|---|---|---|
| 売上 | $800,000 | $200,000 |
| 売上原価 | $490,000 | $144,000 |

20X0年にプライム社は原価 $40,000 の商品をサン社に $50,000 で販売した。20X0年12月31日時点では、この商品の 1/4 がサン社の棚卸資産に含まれていた。

### 18-4

20X0年におけるプライム社とサン社の連結売上高はいくらか。

(1) $ 950,000

(2) $ 960,000

(3) $ 987,500

(4) $ 990,000

(5) $1,000,000

**解答　（1）**

**解説** ……………………………………………………… 公式テキスト Chapter18-8

連結会社間の商品売買取引は相殺消去される。プライム社の売上高は $50,000 なのでサン社の仕入高も $50,000 となる。そのためこの $50,000 を消去する。

Dr Sales　　　　　　　　　　　　　50,000

　　Cr Cost of sales　　　　　　　　　　　　50,000

よって連結売上高は、

$ 800,000 + $200,000 − $50,000 = $950,000

# Business Combinations / Consolidated Statements

## 18-5

20X0年におけるプライム社とサン社の連結売上原価はいくらか。

(1) $586,500

(2) $591,500

(3) $594,000

(4) $624,000

(5) $634,000

**解答　(1)**

**解説** ...................................................... 公式テキスト Chapter18-8

連結会社間での商品売買取引で、プライム社が利益を計上してもサン社が外部に販売しない限り、この利益は実現できない。そこで期末にサン社の棚卸資産の中に含まれている未実現利益を消去する必要がある。

全体の売上総利益は、$50,000 − $40,000 = $10,000で、このうちの1/4である$2,500が期末の棚卸資産に含まれている。この未実現利益を消去すると、

Dr  Cost of sales　　　　　　　2,500
　　Cr Inventory　　　　　　　　　　　　2,500

設問では連結の Cost of sales の金額を問われているので、プライム社とサン社の合計額から売買取引分と未実現利益分を調整して求める。

$490,000 + $144,000 − $50,000 + $2,500 = $586,500

## Business Combinations / Consolidated Statements

### 18-6

以下はパラダイス社と同社が株式80％を所有している子会社サン社の20X0年12月31日に終了する会計年度の損益計算書である。

| | パラダイス社 | サン社 |
|---|---|---|
| 売上 | $800,000 | $200,000 |
| 売上原価 | 490,000 | 144,000 |
| 売上総利益 | 310,000 | 56,000 |
| 費用 | 160,000 | 36,000 |
| 当期純利益 | $150,000 | $ 20,000 |

20X0年にサン社は原価 $40,000 の商品をパラダイス社に $50,000 で販売した。20X0年12月31日時点では、この商品の1/4がパラダイス社の棚卸資産に含まれていた。

20X0年の連結損益計算書に計上すべき金額を計算しなさい。

(a) 非支配持分に帰する利益

(b) 売上高

(c) 売上原価

(d) 親会社の所有者に帰する利益

## Business Combinations / Consolidated Statements

解答　(a) $ 　3,500
　　　(b) $950,000
　　　(c) $586,500
　　　(d) $164,000

解説 ……………………………………………………………… 公式テキスト Chapter18-8

この設問は前述の問題がダウン・ストリーム（親会社から子会社への販売）
であったのに対して、アップ・ストリーム（子会社から親会社への販売）で
未実現利益が発生したケースである。

(a) 前問から $2,500（$10,000×1/4）の未実現利益を、20％の非支配持分に負
　　担させるため、非支配持分に帰する利益は、（子会社当期純利益 $20,000
　　−未実現利益 $2,500）×20％ = $3,500 となる。

(b) $800,000 + $200,000 − $50,000（連結会社間取引）= $950,000

(c) $490,000 + $144,000 + 2,500（未実現利益）− 50,000（連結会社間取引）
　　=$586,500

(d) $950,000 − $586,500 − $196,000 − $3,500 = $164,000

Chapter 18

**231**

## Business Combinations / Consolidated Statements

### 18-7

20X2年1月1日、P社はS社の持分の80%を現金$400,000で取得した。

20X2年1月1日におけるS社の資産の公正価値と簿価は次のようになっている。

|  | 簿価 | 公正価値 |
|---|---|---|
| 棚卸資産 | $ 30,000 | $ 40,000 |
| 建物 | 200,000 | 250,000 |
| 設備 | 100,000 | 130,000 |
| 機械 | 150,000 | 170,000 |
| その他資産 | 50,000 | 70,000 |

20X2年1月1日における非支配持分の公正価値は$90,000であった。P社はS社の非支配持分を公正価値で測定することを選択した。

Business Combinations / Consolidated Statements

消去仕訳を行い、合併直後の下記の精算表を完成させなさい。

下記の精算表の最初の2列はP社とS社の取得直後の帳簿の数字である。

取得日の連結精算表 ($)

| | P社 | S社 | 消去・修正仕訳 (借) | (貸) | 非支配持分 (借) | (貸) | 連結 残高 |
|---|---|---|---|---|---|---|---|
| 現金 | 300,000 | 50,000 | | | | | |
| 売掛金 | 130,000 | 160,000 | | | | | |
| 棚卸商品 | 114,000 | 30,000 | | | | | |
| 建物 | 400,000 | 200,000 | | | | | |
| 設備 | 200,000 | 100,000 | | | | | |
| 機械 | 250,000 | 150,000 | | | | | |
| S社への投資 | 400,000 | | | | | | |
| 投資有価証券 | 0 | 100,000 | | | | | |
| その他資産 | 120,000 | 50,000 | | | | | |
| のれん | | | | | | | |
| 資産合計 | 1,914,000 | 840,000 | | | | | |
| 短期借入金 | 120,000 | 70,000 | | | | | |
| 買掛金 | 150,000 | 95,000 | | | | | |
| 長期借入金 | 100,000 | 155,000 | | | | | |
| 社債 | 320,000 | 220,000 | | | | | |
| 資本金 | 700,000 | 150,000 | | | | | |
| 資本剰余金 | 200,000 | 50,000 | | | | | |
| 利益剰余金 | 324,000 | 100,000 | | | | | |
| 非支配持分 | | | | | | | |
| 負債・資本合計 | 1,914,000 | 840,000 | | | | | |

233

## Business Combinations / Consolidated Statements

## 解答

### Consolidation Working Paper at Date of Acquisition ($)

| | P Company | S Company | Adjustment and Elimination Dr | Adjustment and Elimination Cr | Non-controlling Interest Dr | Non-controlling Interest Cr | Consolidated Balances |
|---|---|---|---|---|---|---|---|
| Cash | 300,000 | 50,000 | | | | | 350,000 |
| Accounts receivable | 130,000 | 160,000 | | | | | 290,000 |
| Inventories | 114,000 | 30,000 | 8,000 | | 2,000 | | 154,000 |
| Buildings | 400,000 | 200,000 | 40,000 | | 10,000 | | 650,000 |
| Equipment | 200,000 | 100,000 | 24,000 | | 6,000 | | 330,000 |
| Machinery | 250,000 | 150,000 | 16,000 | | 4,000 | | 420,000 |
| Investment in S | 400,000 | | | 400,000 | | | 0 |
| Investment | 0 | 100,000 | | | | | 100,000 |
| Other assets | 120,000 | 50,000 | 16,000 | | 4,000 | | 190,000 |
| Goodwill | | | 56,000 | | 4,000 | | 60,000 |
| Total Assets | 1,914,000 | 840,000 | 160,000 | 400,000 | 30,000 | 0 | 2,544,000 |
| Short-term borrowings | 120,000 | 70,000 | | | | | 190,000 |
| Accounts payable | 150,000 | 95,000 | | | | | 245,000 |
| Long-term debt | 100,000 | 155,000 | | | | | 255,000 |
| Bonds | 320,000 | 220,000 | | | | | 540,000 |
| Share capital | 700,000 | 150,000 | 120,000 | | 30,000 | | 700,000 |
| Share premium | 200,000 | 50,000 | 40,000 | | 10,000 | | 200,000 |
| Retained earnings | 324,000 | 100,000 | 80,000 | | 20,000 | | 324,000 |
| Non-controlling interest | | | | | | 90,000 | 90,000 |
| Total Liabilities and Equity | 1,914,000 | 840,000 | 240,000 | | 60,000 | 90,000 | 2,544,000 |

### 解説 ································· 公式テキスト Chapter18-6

仕訳は以下のとおりとなる。

〈STEP1〉

P 社の投資勘定と S 社の資本勘定を相殺する。親会社持分（80%）について、S 社の資産・負債を帳簿価額から公正価値に修正し、親会社持分に帰するのれんを認識する。

Business Combinations / Consolidated Statements

```
Dr Share capital          120,000
   Share premium           40,000
   Retained earnings       80,000
   Inventories              8,000
   Buildings               40,000
   Equipment               24,000
   Machinery               16,000
   Other assets            16,000
   Goodwill                56,000
   Cr Investment in S                    400,000
```

〈STEP2〉

S社の第三者株主持分を非支配持分につけかえる。非支配持分（20%）について、S社の資産・負債を帳簿価額から公正価値に修正し、非支配持分に帰するのれんを認識する。

```
Dr Share capital           30,000
   Share premium           10,000
   Retained earnings       20,000
   Inventories              2,000
   Buildings               10,000
   Equipment                6,000
   Machinery                4,000
   Other assets             4,000
   Goodwill                 4,000
   Cr Non-controlling interest            90,000
```

Chapter 18

## Business Combinations / Consolidated Statements

### 18-8

20X2年10月1日、横浜㈱は港㈱の発行済株式1,000株のうち350株を¥5,250,000で購入した。港の20X2年度の利益は¥400,000であった。のれんの減損はないと仮定すれば、20X2年12月31日の財政状態計算書において、横浜は港への投資としていくらを報告すべきか。

(1) ¥4,585,000

(2) ¥5,250,000

(3) ¥5,285,000

(4) ¥5,390,000

(5) ¥5,650,000

解答　(3)

解説 ································································· 公式テキスト Chapter18-4

20X2年10月1日の仕訳

Dr Investment　　　　　　　　　　5,250,000

　　Cr Cash　　　　　　　　　　　　　　　5,250,000

20X2年12月31日の仕訳

Dr Investment　　　　　　　　　35,000

　　Cr Equity income from investment　　　　35,000

　　(¥400,000×3/12×35% = ¥35,000)

Investment = ¥5,250,000 + ¥35,000 = ¥5,285,000

解答編

**CHAPTER 19**

# The Effects of Changes in
# Foreign Exchange Rates

Bookkeeping & Accounting Test for International Communication

# BATIC
Bookkeeper & Accountant Level

## The Effects of Changes in Foreign Exchange Rates

### 19-1

ある外国の子会社の機能通貨は、その会社の所在国の現地通貨である。子会社の試算表を機能通貨から表示通貨へと換算する。次の各項目はどの換算レートを使って、換算すべきか。

(a) 現金
(b) 機械装置
(c) 棚卸資産
(d) 売上
(e) 広告費


① 期末日レート
② 取引日レート
③ その年の加重平均レート


**解答**　(a) ①
　　　　　(b) ①
　　　　　(c) ①
　　　　　(d) ②
　　　　　(e) ②

**解説** ……………………………………………………… 公式テキスト Chapter19-3

機能通貨から表示通貨に換算する場合、資産・負債は期末日レート（closing rate）を使用し、収益・費用は各取引日のレートを使用する。なお、収益・費用については期中の平均レートを用いても良いが、変動が大きい場合は不可とされているため、③は誤りとなる。

The Effects of Changes in Foreign Exchange Rates

**問題 2 から 4 は、以下に基づく。**

ある日本企業の豪州子会社は 20X4 年 1 月 1 日に現金 $80,000 に対し株式を発行して設立された。子会社の機能通貨及び表示通貨は日本円である。

20X4 年に下記の取引があった。

| 日付 | 取引 | 為替レート |
|---|---|---|
| 1 月 1 日 | 現金 $80,000 に対して株式を発行した。 | $1 = ¥92 |
| 3 月 31 日 | 現金 $40,000 で費用の支払いを行った。 | $1 = ¥93 |
| 7 月 1 日 | サービスを提供し現金 $50,000 を受け取った。 | $1 = ¥96 |
| 10 月 1 日 | サービスを提供し現金 $20,000 を受け取った。 | $1 = ¥97 |
| 12 月 10 日 | 現金 $25,000 でオフィス備品*を購入した。 | $1 = ¥98 |
| 12 月 31 日 | — | $1 = ¥95 |

*経営陣はオフィス備品を原価で測定する選択を行った。減価償却は無視せよ。

### 19-2

20X4 年 12 月 31 日に終了する年度の子会社の損益計算書において、サービスからの収益をいくら認識すべきか。

**解答　¥6,740,000**

解説 ················································· 公式テキスト Chapter19-3

収益は取引時のレートで測定する。
$50,000 × 96 = ¥4,800,000$
$20,000 × 97 = ¥1,940,000$
　　　　　　　¥6,740,000

Chapter 19

# The Effects of Changes in Foreign Exchange Rates

## 19-3

20X4年12月31日現在の子会社の財政状態計算書において、幾らの現金を記録すべきか。

**解答**　¥8,075,000

**解説** ・・・・・・・・・・・・・・・・・・・・・・・・・・・・・・・・・・・・・・・・・・・・・・・・・・・・・・・ 公式テキスト Chapter19-3

期末時点の現金残高：$80,000 − $40,000 + $50,000 + $20,000 − $25,000 = $85,000

貨幣項目は期末時の為替レートで再測定しなければならないため、

$85,000 × 95 = ¥8,075,000

となる。

The Effects of Changes in Foreign Exchange Rates

## 19-4

20X4年12月31日に終了する年度の子会社の損益計算書において、利益をいくら認識すべきか。

**解答** ¥3,165,000

**解説** ················································· 公式テキスト Chapter19-3

費用は $40,000×93 = ¥3,720,000

また現金の換算差額が以下のとおり発生している。

Cash（¥）

| | | | |
|---|---|---|---|
| 1/1 | 7,360,000 | 3/31 | 3,720,000 |
| 7/1 | 4,800,000 | 12/10 | 2,450,000 |
| 10/1 | 1,940,000 | | |
| （差額） | 145,000 | | |
| 12/31 | 8,075,000 | | |

したがって、利益は ¥6,740,000 − ¥3,720,000 + ¥145,000 = ¥3,165,000

＜参考＞

財政状態計算書

| | $ | 為替レート | ¥ |
|---|---|---|---|
| 資産： | | | |
| 現金 | 85,000 | 95 | 8,075,000 |
| オフィス備品 | 25,000 | 98 | 2,450,000 |
| 合計 | 110,000 | | 10,525,000 |
| 負債及び資本： | | | |
| 資本金 | 80,000 | 92 | 7,360,000 |
| 利益剰余金 | 30,000 | — | 3,165,000 |
| 合計 | 110,000 | | 10,525,000 |

損益計算書

| | | | |
|---|---|---|---|
| 収益 | 70,000 | — | 6,740,000 |
| 費用 | 40,000 | 93 | 3,720,000 |
| 換算差額 | | | 145,000 |
| 利益 | 30,000 | | 3,165,000 |

Chapter 19

241

解答編

**CHAPTER 20**

# Accounting Policies, Changes in Accounting Estimates and Errors

Bookkeeping & Accounting Test for International Communication

# BATIC

Bookkeeper & Accountant Level

## Accounting Policies, Changes in Accounting Estimates and Errors

### 20-1

マックス社は棚卸資産の会計方針に棚卸計算法を使った先入先出法を採用している。20X2年度中にマックス社は20X0年と20X1年の財務諸表に記載されている期末棚卸資産が以下のように誤って記載されていることを発見した。

20X0年　€20,000の過大計上
20X1年　€ 5,000の過小計上

これらの誤謬の訂正がなされる前、マックス社の20X2年度利益剰余金の期首残高は、

(1) 影響なし
(2) € 5,000の過小計上
(3) €15,000の過小計上
(4) €15,000に過大計上
(5) 上記のいずれでもない

### 解答　(2)

**解説** ……………………………………………………… 公式テキスト Chapter20-4

20X0年の棚卸資産の過大計上は20X2年1月1日までに解消される(20X0年の当期純利益が過大計上され,20X1年の当期純利益が過小計上される)。一方、20X1年の棚卸資産の過小計上は、20X1年の当期純利益と20X2年の利益剰余金の期首残高とを過小計上させる。

## Accounting Policies, Changes in Accounting Estimates and Errors

**20-2**

ラックス社は 20X0 年度中に会計処理を IFRS に準拠しない会計方針から準拠する
ものへと変更した。ラックス社はこの変更の影響をどのように報告すべきか。

(1) 異常項目

(2) 会計方針の変更による修正再表示

(3) 誤謬の訂正による修正再表示

(4) 法人税

(5) 上記のいずれでもない

**解答　(3)**

解説‥‥‥‥‥‥‥‥‥‥‥‥‥‥‥‥‥‥‥‥‥‥‥‥　公式テキスト Chapter20-4

IFRS に準拠しない会計方針の適用は誤謬（error）である。誤謬の場合は、
原則として遡及的に財務諸表を修正しなくてはならない。

## Accounting Policies, Changes in Accounting Estimates and Errors

### 20-3

20X0年1月1日、タワー社は見積耐用年数10年で残存価額ゼロの機械を$500,000で購入した。機械の減価償却は定額法によって行われている。20X2年1月1日にタワー社は、この機械の耐用年数は取得日から起算して6年であり、残存価額は$40,000であると再見積りを行った。この変更の結果、20X2年12月31日においてタワー社が認識すべき機械の減価償却累計額はいくらか。

(1) $230,000

(2) $200,000

(3) $190,000

(4) $150,000

(5) 上記のいずれでもない

### 解答 (3)

#### 解説 ......................................................... 公式テキスト Chapter20-3

会計上の見積りの変更は、当期および翌期以降にわたって会計処理されなければならない。20X0年と20X1年の減価償却費は$50,000(＝$500,000÷10年)であった。よって、20X1年12月31日における減価償却累計額と簿価は、それぞれ$100,000と$400,000となる。20X2年1月1日にタワー社は、耐用年数を取得日から6年、残存価額をゼロから$40,000へと変更した。よって当期以降は、償却可能価額$360,000(＝$400,000－$40,000)を残りの耐用年数4年にわたって償却しなければならない。20X2年度の減価償却費は$90,000（＝$360,000÷4年)となり、20X2年12月31日における減価償却累計額は$190,000(＝$100,000＋$90,000)と報告されなければならない。

## Accounting Policies, Changes in Accounting Estimates and Errors

### 20-4

20X6年にオーウェン社は、会計方針の変更を行った。実務上不可能でないならば、オーウェン社は、

a. 20X6年の損益計算書に会計方針の変更による累積的影響額として含める。

b. 新しい会計方針を前期から遡及的に適用する。

c. 新しい会計方針を過年度全てに遡及的に適用する。

(1) a. のみ

(2) b. のみ

(3) c. のみ

(4) a. か b. のみ

(5) a. か c. のみ

### 解答　(3)

解説 ……………………………………………………………… 公式テキスト Chapter20-2

会計方針の変更は、遡及適用（retrospective application）であり、実務上不可能でない場合は、公表される最も古い財務諸表の期首残高を修正し、その他の全ての財務諸表の対応する金額を修正しなければならない。

解答編

**CHAPTER 21**

Earnings per Share

Bookkeeping & Accounting Test for International Communication

BATIC

Bookkeeper & Accountant Level

# Earnings per Share

## 21-1

20X0年度中のジョー社の資本構成は以下のとおりであった。

| | |
|---|---|
| 普通株式、額面 $25、流通株式 4,000,000 株 | $100,000,000 |
| 転換優先株式、額面 $15、非累積的、流通株式 500,000 株 | $ 7,500,000 |

転換優先株式は普通株式 1,000,000 株に転換できる。20X0年度のジョー社の当期純利益は $47,500,000 で、優先株 1 株につき $5 の配当宣言をおこなった。20X0年度の包括利益計算書においてジョー社が報告すべき希薄化後 1 株当たり利益はいくらか。

(1) $ 8.50

(2) $ 9.50

(3) $11.25

(4) $12.90

(5) 上記のいずれでもない

### 解答 （2）

解説 ･･････････････････････････････････････････ 公式テキスト Chapter21-3

もし転換優先株式が全て普通株式に転換されたとすると、分子が優先配当額 $2,500,000 分増加し（$5×500,000 株）、分母の普通株式数が 1,000,000 株増加する。1 株当たり利益を $11.25 から $9.5 に減少させるので、この転換優先株式は希薄化効果がある。

基本的 1 株当たり利益：

$$\frac{当期純利益\ \$47,500,000\ -\ 優先株配当金\ \$2,500,000}{流通普通株式\ 4,000,000\ 株} = \$11.25$$

希薄化後 1 株当たり利益：

$$\frac{\$47,500,000\ -\ \$2,500,000\ +\ \$2,500,000}{4,000,000\ 株\ +\ 1,000,000\ 株} = \$9.50$$

Chapter 21

# Earnings per Share

**問題 2 および 3 は以下に基づく。**

次の情報は ABC 社の資本構成に関するものである。

普通株式
額面€10の普通株式、20X0年1月1日～20X0年12月31日　　10,000株

優先株式
額面€5、8%の累積的転換優先株式、20X0年1月1日～20X0年12月31日　　2,000株
1株が普通株式2株に転換できる。

20X0年の当期純利益
€70,000

## 21-2

20X0年12月31日に終了する年度に、ABC社は基本的一株あたり利益としていくら報告すべきか。金額は小数点第2位まで四捨五入すること。

(1) €5.00

(2) €6.73

(3) €6.92

(4) €7.00

(5) €7.08

**解答　(3)**

解説 ・・・・・・・・・・・・・・・・・・・・・・・・・・・・・・・・・・・・・・・・・・・・・・・・・・・・　公式テキスト Chapter21-2

$$\frac{€70,000 - €5 \times 2,000\ 株 \times 8\%}{10,000\ 株} = €6.92$$

**251**

**Earnings per Share**

## 21-3

20X0年12月31日に終了する年度に、ABC社は希薄化後一株あたり利益としていくら報告すべきか。金額は小数点第2位まで四捨五入すること。

(1) €5.00

(2) €6.73

(3) €6.92

(4) €7.00

(5) €7.08

**解答　(1)**

**解説** ・・・・・・・・・・・・・・・・・・・・・・・・・・・・・・・・・・・・・・・・・・・・・・・・・・・・・・・・・ 公式テキスト Chapter21-3

優先株式が普通株式に転換されたと仮定して、算出する。

$$\frac{€70,000}{10,000株 + 4,000株} = €5.00$$

解答編

**CHAPTER 22**

# Interim Financial
# Reporting

Bookkeeping & Accounting Test for International Communication

# BATIC

Bookkeeper & Accountant Level

**Interim Financial Reporting**

## 22-1

以下の空欄を埋める最も適当な番号を選べ。

企業は、年次財務報告と比較して、期中財務報告に含める情報をより少なく提供してもよい。その理由の一つは、□□□□□□□□のためである。

(1) 比較可能性
(2) 目的適合性
(3) 信頼性
(4) 適時性
(5) 検証可能性

**解答　(4)**

**解説** ·········································· 公式テキスト Chapter22-1

期中財務報告は、財務諸表利用者の意思決定に役立つように、より迅速な開示すなわち適時性（timeliness）が重視されている。

**Interim Financial Reporting**

## 22-2

1月にグリーン社は第二四半期に€40,000のコストが発生する年間の従業員トレーニングプログラムを計画した。プログラムは実際に第二四半期に行われた。

各四半期包括利益計算書において、いくらの費用を計上すべきか。

| | 第一四半期 | 第二四半期 | 第三四半期 | 第四四半期 |
|---|---|---|---|---|
| (1) | €0 | €0 | €20,000 | €20,000 |
| (2) | €0 | €40,000 | €0 | €0 |
| (3) | €10,000 | €10,000 | €10,000 | €10,000 |
| (4) | €20,000 | €20,000 | €0 | €0 |
| (5) | €40,000 | €0 | €0 | €0 |

**解答　(2)**

**解説** ……………………………………………………… 公式テキスト Chapter22-2

発生時に全額認識し、見越・繰延処理はできない。

解答編

# CHAPTER 23

## Operating Segments

Bookkeeping & Accounting Test for International Communication

# BATIC
Bookkeeper & Accountant Level

## Operating Segments

### 23-1

下記の情報はイエロー社の6つの事業セグメントに関するものである。

| セグメント | 売上高合計 * | 内部売上 | 営業利益 | (百万円) 資産 |
|---|---|---|---|---|
| A | 40 | | 20 | 10 |
| B | 120 | | 40 | 80 |
| C | 350 | 200 | 80 | 120 |
| D | 500 | 250 | (150) | 200 |
| E | 600 | 100 | 230 | 200 |
| F | 1,000 | 300 | 280 | 600 |
| Total | 2,610 | 850 | 500 | 1,210 |

\* 売上高合計は内部売上を含む。

イエロー社の報告セグメントは

(1) A, B, C, D, E, F

(2) B, C, D, E, F

(3) C, D, E, F

(4) D, E, F

(5) E, F

## Operating Segments

## 解答　(3)

**解説** ·········································· 公式テキスト Chapter23-2

ステップ1：

①売上高テスト　　2,610×10% ＝ 261　　　→C、D、E、Fが満たす。

②営業利益テスト　20 ＋ 40 ＋ 80 ＋ 230 ＋ 280 ＝ 650>150

　　　　　　　　　650×10% ＝ 65　　　→C、D、E、Fが満たす。

③資産テスト　　　1,210×10% ＝ 121　　　→D、E、Fが満たす。

以上よりC、D、E、Fが報告セグメントの候補となる。

ステップ2：

報告セグメントの内部売上を除いた売上高合計が連結売上高合計の75%
以上でなくてはならない。

(2,610 － 850)×75% ＝ 1,320

(350 － 200) ＋ (500 － 250) ＋ (600 － 100) ＋ (1,000 － 300) ＝ 1,600

1,600 ＞ 1,320なのでテストをクリアしている。

**Operating Segments**

## 23-2

次の情報は ABC 社の 6 つの事業セグメントに関するものである。

| セグメント | 売上高合計* | 内部売上 | 営業利益 | 資産 |
|---|---|---|---|---|
| A | $10,000 | $1,000 | $300 | $10,000 |
| B | 7,000 | 1,500 | 150 | 10,000 |
| C | 5,000 | 2,000 | 120 | 3,000 |
| D | 4,000 | 2,000 | 30 | 2,000 |
| E | 2,000 | 1,500 | 50 | 1,000 |
| F | 1,000 | 500 | 50 | 500 |
| Total | $29,000 | $8,500 | $700 | $26,500 |

*売上高合計は内部売上を含む。

ABC 社は報告セグメントをいくつ持っているか。

(1) 2つ

(2) 3つ

(3) 4つ

(4) 5つ

(5) 6つ

### 解答　(3)

**解説** ……………………………………………… 公式テキスト Chapter23-2

ステップ1

①売上高テスト　　$29,000 × 10\% = \$2,900$ → A, B, C, D が満たす。

②営業利益テスト　$700 × 10\% = \$70$　　　 → A, B, C が満たす。

③資産テスト　　　$26,500 × 10\% = \$2,650$ → A, B, C が満たす。

以上より A, B, C, D が報告セグメントの候補となる。

ステップ2

内部売上を除いた全売上高合計 = $(\$29,000 - \$8,500) × 75\% = \$15,375$

A, B, C, D の内部売上を除いた売上高合計 = $\$10,000 - \$1,000 + \$7,000 - \$1,500 + \$5,000 - \$2,000 + \$4,000 - \$2,000 = \$19,500$ となり、上記金額を超えるので、そのまま、A, B, C, D が報告セグメントとなる。

解答編

## Appendix

# Time Value of Money

Bookkeeping & Accounting Test for International Communication

# BATIC
Bookkeeper & Accountant Level

# Time Value of Money

## A-1

20X2年11月30日に、ジェームス社は工業機械をアダムス社に売った。その代金として、ジェームス社は、5年間にわたって毎年$20,000ずつ支払うことを約定した無利息の手形を、アダムス社から受け取った。アダムス社の第一回目の支払いは20X3年11月30日である。この手形の発行日時点での、同様な手形の市場利回りは8%であった。以下は現在価値に関する情報である。

| | |
|---|---:|
| $1を複利8%で4年間運用した場合の現在価値 | $0.74 |
| $1を複利8%で5年間運用した場合の現在価値 | 0.68 |
| $1の期末年金を複利8%で4年間運用した場合の現在価値 | 3.31 |
| $1の期末年金を複利8%で5年間運用した場合の現在価値 | 3.99 |

20X2年11月30日に、ジェームス社は受取手形としていくら記帳すべきか。

(1) $66,200

(2) $71,500

(3) $79,800

(4) $86,200

(5) 上記のいずれでもない

## 解答 (3)

**解説** ................................................................ 公式テキストAppendix

この例では、第一回目の支払いが、手形発行の一年後に行われるので、期末年金となる。よって、20X2年11月30日に記帳されるべき受取手形の金額は、$79,800（＝$20,000×3.99 Present value of an ordinary annuity of $1 at 8% for 5 periods）となる。

## Time Value of Money

### A-2

$100,000 を年利率が 8%、5 年間で運用する場合に、次のうちどの時間価値の概念が最も高い金額を表すか。

(1) 年利率が8%で5年間の期首年金の現在価値

(2) 年利率が8%で5年間の期末年金の将来価値

(3) 年利率が8%で5年間の将来価値

(4) 年利率が8%で5年間の現在価値

(5) 年利率が8%で5年間の期末年金の現在価値

**解答　(2)**

**解説** ·················································· 公式テキスト Appendix

年利率が8%で5年間の各々の時間価値は、(1)4.31213、(2)5.86660、(3)1.46933、(4)0.68058、(5)3.99271 となり、この値に $100,000 を掛けて各時間価値を求める。たとえば (1) は $100,000 × 4.31213 = $431,213 となる。以下 (2) $586,660、(3) $146,933、(4) $68,058、(5) $399,271 となる。

過去問題

# 第37回 試験問題

検定試験実施時の問題をそのまま掲載しています。

Bookkeeping & Accounting Test for International Communication

# BATIC

Bookkeeper & Accountant Level

第37回 試験問題

Fiscal years of the companies in this test are from 1 January to 31 December.

**1** Select the most appropriate combination to fill in the following blanks.

The fundamental qualitative characteristics of useful financial information are
[    A    ] and [    B    ]. [    A    ] describes the capability to make
a difference in the decisions of users of financial information. To be a [    B    ], a
depiction of economic phenomenon would be complete, neutral and free from error.

| A | B |
|---|---|
| ① Relevance | Comparative information |
| ② Relevance | Faithful representation |
| ③ Relevance | Reasonable assurance |
| ④ Understandability | Comparative information |
| ⑤ Understandability | Faithful representation |

**2** The following information is available to prepare current assets section of ABC Company's statement of financial position as at 31 December 2018.

| | |
|---|---:|
| Bank overdrafts which are an integral part of ABC Company's cash management | $ 27,000 |
| Investments in associates held for the purpose other than trading | 52,000 |
| Investments in equity securities held for the purpose of trading | 28,000 |
| Merchandise inventories expected to be sold in the normal operating cycle | 46,000 |
| Trade receivables expected to be settled in the normal operating cycle | 95,000 |
| Unrestricted cash and cash equivalents | 160,000 |

What amount should ABC Company present in current assets section of its statement of financial position as at 31 December 2018?

① $302,000
② $326,000
③ $329,000
④ $353,000
⑤ $356,000

266

第37回 試験問題

**3** XYZ Company measures the expected credit losses of accounts receivable which do not have a significant financing component using a provision matrix. On 31 December 2018, it estimated the following provision matrix in accordance with IFRS 9.

| Days past due | Gross carrying amount of accounts receivable | Default rate |
|---|---|---|
| Current | €120,000 | 2% |
| 1-45 days | 18,000 | 5% |
| 46-90 days | 8,000 | 15% |
| Over 90 days | 5,000 | 30% |

Additional information is as follows:
- On 1 January 2018, loss allowance for expected credit losses was €7,000.
- During 2018, XYZ Company wrote off €6,200 of accounts receivable which was recorded last year.

Which journal entry should XYZ Company make for the loss allowance on 31 December 2018?

① Dr Loss allowance             800
　　Cr Accounts receivable               800
② Dr Loss allowance           6,000
　　Cr Accounts receivable            6,000
③ Dr Impairment loss         5,200
　　Cr Loss allowance             5,200
④ Dr Impairment loss         6,000
　　Cr Loss allowance             6,000
⑤ Dr Impairment loss         6,200
　　Cr Loss allowance             6,200

第37回 試験問題

Questions **4** and **5** are based on the following:

ABC Company had the following information relating to its merchandise inventory during 2018.

|  | Units | Unit cost |
|---|---|---|
| 1 January, beginning balance | 3,000 | $12 |
| 2 March, sold | 2,000 | |
| 10 April, purchased | 4,000 | $14 |
| 26 June, sold | 1,500 | |
| 5 September, sold | 2,500 | |
| 17 October, purchased | 4,000 | $16 |
| 21 December, sold | 1,500 | |

On 31 December 2018, the following information was available relating to the merchandise inventory.

| Estimated selling price per unit | $25 |
|---|---|
| Estimated cost to sell per unit | 13 |
| Replacement cost per unit | 17 |

ABC Company uses a perpetual method and the first-in, first-out method.

**4** What amount is the cost of the merchandise inventory before being measured at the lower of cost and net realisable value as at 31 December 2018?

① $42,000
② $49,000
③ $54,320
④ $56,000
⑤ $59,500

**5** What amount of write-down of inventories to net realisable value relating to the merchandise inventory should ABC Company recognise for the year ended 31 December 2018?

① $0
② $ 3,500
③ $12,320
④ $14,000
⑤ $17,500

268

第37回 試験問題

Questions **6** and **7** are based on the following:

On 1 January 2016, XYZ Company acquired and started to use a machine for the production of goods. On the same date, the following expenditures were incurred relating to the machine.

| | |
|---|---|
| Purchase price | €45,000 |
| Freight and insurance costs | 1,800 |
| Installation and assembly costs | 1,200 |

For 2016 through 2018, it paid the following repair costs to maintain the machine in the operating condition.

| 2016 | 2017 | 2018 |
|---|---|---|
| €900 | €1,200 | €1,500 |

On 31 December 2018, it sold the machine for €23,000 cash.

Additional information is as follows:
- XYZ Company used a cost model for the machine which had a six-year useful life and no residual value and was depreciated using the straight-line method.
- XYZ Company did not change the useful life, the residual value and the depreciation method of the machine for 2016 through 2018.
- The machine was not expected to be sold before 2018.
- XYZ Company did not recognise any impairment loss for 2016 through 2018.

**6** What is the carrying amount of the machine as at 31 December 2016?

① €37,500
② €38,500
③ €39,000
④ €40,000
⑤ €40,750

**7** What amount of gain or loss should XYZ Company recognise in its 2018 financial statements as a result of the sale of the machine?

① €3,295 of loss
② €1,440 of loss
③ €1,000 of loss
④ €500 of gain
⑤ €1,000 of gain

269

**8** Company A contracted with Company B to construct its own warehouse for $600,000 on 1 September 2017. The construction began immediately and completed on 31 October 2018.

Company A paid the following amounts for the construction to Company B.

| | |
|---|---|
| 1 September 2017 | $200,000 |
| 31 October 2018 | 400,000 |

To finance the above payments, Company A has the following loan from a bank.

| Borrowing date | Amount | Annual interest | Principal repayment date |
|---|---|---|---|
| 1 September 2017 | $600,000 | 5% | 31 August 2020 |

Between 1 September 2017 and 31 October 2018, Company A temporarily invested $400,000 of the remainder of the borrowing after the first payment and earned $17,000 of interest revenue. The warehouse is a qualifying asset.

What amount of borrowing costs should be included in the acquisition cost of the warehouse as at 31 December 2018?

① $0
② $18,000
③ $23,000
④ $35,000
⑤ $40,000

270

**第37回 試験問題**

**9** On 1 January 2016, XYZ Company purchased manufacturing equipment at a cost of €490,000. It keeps accounting records of the equipment based on the significant components and depreciates them separately. The following information relates to the significant components of the equipment.

| | Acquisition date | Acquisition cost | Useful life | Residual value |
|---|---|---|---|---|
| Component A | 1 January 2016 | €250,000 | 10 years | €0 |
| Component B | 1 January 2016 | 150,000 | 6 years | 0 |
| Component C | 1 January 2016 | 90,000 | 3 years | 0 |

On 31 December 2018, XYZ Company replaced the component C to a new one costing €80,000.

XYZ Company adopts the cost model and uses the straight-line method for all of the above components.

What is the total carrying amount of the equipment as at 31 December 2018?

① €175,000
② €250,000
③ €330,000
④ €343,000
⑤ €423,000

**10** The following is a description regarding intangible assets. Select the most appropriate combination to fill in the blanks.

If an intangible resource which a company acquired does not meet the definition of intangible assets, that is, ⬚ A ⬚ , ⬚ B ⬚ over the resource and existence of ⬚ C ⬚ , expenditure to acquire the intangible resource is recognised as an expense.

| | A | B | C |
|---|---|---|---|
| ① | Identifiability | Concern | Cash flow |
| ② | Identifiability | Control | Future economic benefits |
| ③ | Identifiability | Control | Possibility of depreciation |
| ④ | Integrity | Control | Cash flow |
| ⑤ | Integrity | Influence | Future economic benefits |

271

第37回 試験問題

**11** ABC Company is being involved in a project to develop a new material. It spent the following expenditures on the new material during 2018.

| | |
|---|---|
| Between 1 January 2018 and 31 August 2018 | $110,000 |
| Between 1 September 2018 and 31 December 2018 | 24,000 |

In addition to the above expenditures, it spent $12,000 on the sales promotion of the material during 2018.

ABC Company can demonstrate that the production know-how of the new material met the criteria for recognition as an intangible asset on 1 September 2018. It did not recognise any impairment loss and amortisation for 2018.

What amount should ABC Company recognise as an intangible asset relating to the project in its 2018 financial statements?

① $  24,000
② $  36,000
③ $110,000
④ $134,000
⑤ $146,000

**12** On 1 January 2018, XYZ Company acquired a copyright for €240,000 and estimated that it would receive economic benefits from the copyright over 20 years. The legal life of the copyright is 30 years.

Additional information is as follows:

- There is neither purchase commitment by any third party nor active market for the copyright.
- The copyright is expected to generate economic benefits evenly over its useful life.
- The estimate of useful life of the copyright did not change during 2018.
- XYZ Company did not recognise any impairment loss for the year ended 31 December 2018.
- XYZ Company uses the cost model to account for intangible assets.

What is the carrying amount of the copyright in XYZ Company's statement of financial position as at 31 December 2018?

① €0
② €228,000
③ €230,400
④ €232,000
⑤ €240,000

第37回 試験問題

Questions **13** through **15** are based on the following:

The following data relate to machinery that ABC Company owns.

| Acquisition date | Acquisition cost | Useful life | Residual value | Depreciation method |
|---|---|---|---|---|
| 1 January 2015 | $70,000 | 6 years | $7,000 | Straight-line |

On 31 December 2017, as there was an indication of impairment, ABC Company performed an impairment test. It estimated that the fair value less cost of disposal of the machinery on 31 December 2017 was $34,000. Relating to the expected future cash flows from the use and disposal of the machinery, the following information was available.

| 2018 | 2019 | 2020 |
|---|---|---|
| $13,000 | $11,000 | $12,000 |

Additional information is as follows:

- The discount rate is 4%.
- ABC Company uses the cost model to account for the machinery.
- The expected future cash flows occur at the end of each year.

**13** Calculate the value in use of the machinery as at 31 December 2017.

① $30,226
② $32,004
③ $33,301
④ $33,338
⑤ $36,000

**14** What amount of impairment loss should ABC Company recognise for the year ended 31 December 2017?

① $  662
② $1,996
③ $2,000
④ $4,500
⑤ $5,162

273

第37回 試験問題

**15** During 2018, there was neither impairment nor reversal of impairment loss. What amount of depreciation expense should ABC Company report for the year ended 31 December 2018?

① $  8,779
② $  9,000
③ $  9,667
④ $10,500
⑤ $12,000

**16** XYZ Company has a cash-generating unit. On 31 December 2018, as there was an indication that the assets of the unit may be impaired, it performed an impairment test for the unit.

On 31 December 2018, the following information was available.

The cash-generating unit
Carrying amount before impairment test     €900,000
Fair value less cost of disposal     740,000
Value in use     680,000

The carrying amounts of identifiable assets of the unit before impairment test
Equipment     €258,000
Factory     430,000
Land     172,000

The carrying amount of the unit before impairment test included goodwill of €40,000.

What amount should XYZ Company recognise as the carrying amount for each identifiable asset after allocating the impairment loss as at 31 December 2018?

| | Equipment | Factory | Land |
|---|---|---|---|
| ① | €238,000 | €410,000 | €152,000 |
| ② | €222,000 | €370,000 | €148,000 |
| ③ | €218,000 | €390,000 | €132,000 |
| ④ | €210,000 | €350,000 | €140,000 |
| ⑤ | €198,000 | €330,000 | €172,000 |

第37回 試験問題

Questions 17 through 19 are based on the following:

XYZ Company, a lessee, leases equipment that will be returned to the lessor at the end of the lease term. XYZ Company applies IFRS 16. The following information relates to the lease contract.

| | |
|---|---|
| Commencement date | 1 January 2018 |
| Lease term | 4 years |
| Estimated useful life of equipment | 5 years |
| Annual lease payment payable at end of each year | €25,000 |
| Residual value guarantee* | €10,000* |
| Interest rate implicit in lease | 5% |

*It is probable that the expected residual value will be greater than the residual value guarantee and XYZ Company expects to pay nothing under the residual value guarantee.

Calculate using the following present value information, if necessary.

| | |
|---|---|
| Present value of 1 for 4 years at 5% | 0.823 |
| Present value of 1 for 5 years at 5% | 0.784 |
| Present value of ordinary annuity of 1 for 4 years at 5% | 3.546 |
| Present value of ordinary annuity of 1 for 5 years at 5% | 4.329 |

17 What amount of right-of-use asset should XYZ Company record at the commencement date?

① €  88,650
② €  96,490
③ €  96,880
④ €109,225
⑤ €117,065

18 What amount of depreciation expense should XYZ Company, using the straight-line method for depreciation, report for the year ended 31 December 2018?

① €17,730
② €19,376
③ €21,845
④ €22,163
⑤ €24,220

275

第37回 試験問題

**19** What amount of lease receivable should the lessor record at the commencement date? The lessor, neither a manufacturer nor a dealer, classifies the lease as a finance lease.

① € 88,650
② € 96,490
③ € 96,880
④ €109,225
⑤ €117,065

**20** ABC Company, a lessee, entered into a lease contract. The following information relates to the lease contract at the commencement date.

| | |
|---|---|
| Present value of lease payments | $50,000 |
| Lease incentive received | 5,000 |
| Initial direct costs incurred by ABC Company | 9,000 |

What amount of right-use asset should ABC Company record at the commencement date?

① $36,000
② $45,000
③ $50,000
④ $54,000
⑤ $59,000

**21** Regarding accounting for sale and leaseback transactions, select the most appropriate combination to fill in the following blanks.

If the transfer of an asset [ A ] the requirement of IFRS 15 to be accounted for as a sale of the asset, the [ B ] recognises the right-of-use asset at the proportion of the previous carrying amount of the asset that relates to the right of use retained by [ B ].

|  | A | B |
|---|---|---|
| ① | Does not satisfy | Buyer-lessee |
| ② | Does not satisfy | Seller-lessee |
| ③ | Satisfies | Buyer-lessee |
| ④ | Satisfies | Buyer-lessor |
| ⑤ | Satisfies | Seller-lessee |

276

第37回 試験問題

Questions 22 and 23 are based on the following:

During 2018, XYZ Company purchased €50,000 equity securities and received €2,000 as cash dividends on the securities. The dividends did not represent a recovery of part of the cost of the investment. At 31 December 2018, the fair value of the securities was €53,000.

22 Assume that XYZ Company classified the securities as measured at fair value through other comprehensive income. How should it report the increase in fair value of the securities and the cash dividends for 2018 financial statements?

|  | Increase in fair value | Cash dividends |
| --- | --- | --- |
| ① | Other comprehensive income | Equity |
| ② | Other comprehensive income | Other comprehensive income |
| ③ | Other comprehensive income | Profit or loss |
| ④ | Profit or loss | Equity |
| ⑤ | Profit or loss | Other comprehensive income |

23 Assume that XYZ Company classified the securities as measured at fair value through profit or loss. What amount of unrealised holding gain should it recognise at 31 December 2018?

① €0
② €1,000
③ €2,000
④ €3,000
⑤ €5,000

277

第37回 試験問題

Questions 24 and 25 are based on the following:

At 31 December 2017, ABC Company purchased a debt instrument which was classified as measured at fair value through other comprehensive income and determined that the debt instrument was not credit-impaired. There was a significant increase in credit risk on the debt instrument at 31 December 2018.

The following are expected credit losses relating to the debt instrument.

|  | 31 December 2017 | 31 December 2018 |
|---|---|---|
| 12-month expected credit loss | $2,000 | $4,000 |
| Lifetime expected credit loss | 5,000 | 8,000 |

24 Which of the following journal entries should ABC Company make at 31 December 2017?

    ① Dr Impairment loss               2,000
        Cr Loss allowance for financial asset        2,000
    ② Dr Impairment loss               5,000
        Cr Loss allowance for financial asset        5,000
    ③ Dr Impairment loss               2,000
        Cr Other comprehensive income          2,000
    ④ Dr Impairment loss               5,000
        Cr Other comprehensive income          5,000
    ⑤ No journal entry is necessary.

25 What amount of impairment loss should ABC Company recognise for the year ended 31 December 2018?

    ① $2,000
    ② $3,000
    ③ $4,000
    ④ $6,000
    ⑤ $8,000

**26** XYZ Company sold its receivable of €70,000 with no recourse and transferred the contractual rights to receive the cash flow of the receivable to a factor. The factor charged 5% of service fee.

Which of the following journal entries should XYZ Company make to record the sale of the receivable?

| | | | |
|---|---|---|---|
| ① Dr Cash | 66,500 | | |
| Cr Payable to factor | | 66,500 | |
| ② Dr Cash | 70,000 | | |
| Cr Payable to factor | | 70,000 | |
| ③ Dr Cash | 66,500 | | |
| Loss on sale of receivable | 3,500 | | |
| Cr Receivable | | 70,000 | |
| ④ Dr Cash | 70,000 | | |
| Loss on sale of receivable | 3,500 | | |
| Cr Receivable | | 73,500 | |

⑤ No journal entry is necessary.

第37回 試験問題

Questions **27** and **28** are based on the following:

ABC Company issued $20,000 of 3% bonds maturing in 2 years at 1 January 2018. The bonds yield 4% and interest is payable annually at 31 December.

ABC Company did not designate the bonds as measured at fair value through profit or loss.

**27** What is the issue price of the bonds?

① $18,491
② $19,623
③ $20,000
④ $20,022
⑤ $20,382

**28** What is the carrying amount of bonds payable that ABC Company should record as at 31 December 2018?

① $19,808
② $19,815
③ $20,000
④ $20,190
⑤ $20,197

**280**

第37回 試験問題

**29** In October 2018, XYZ Company was sued by a group of former employees seeking €2,000,000 in compensation for health damage caused by poor working conditions. Up to the date of authorisation for issue of its financial statements for 2018, XYZ Company's lawyer advised that it was probable that XYZ Company would lose the lawsuit and the best estimate amount to pay would be €1,000,000. By taking account of all available evidences including the lawyer's advice, XYZ Company determined that it was more likely than not that there was a present obligation at the end of 2018.

Which of the following treatments is XYZ Company required to make for its financial statements for 2018?

① Recognise €1,000,000 as a liability in the statement of financial position.
② Recognise €2,000,000 as a liability in the statement of financial position.
③ Recognise no liability in the financial position but disclose a brief description of the amount of €1,000,000 in the note.
④ Recognise no liability in the financial position but disclose a brief description of the amount of €2,000,000 in the note.
⑤ XYZ Company is not required to recognise any liability in the statement of financial position nor disclose any description in the note.

過去問題

**281**

第37回 試験問題

**30** ABC Company sells a number of products and provides a warranty with all of them. Customers do not have the option to purchase the warranty separately. The warranty does not provide the customers with any service in addition to the assurance that the products comply with agreed-upon specifications.

As at 31 December 2018, ABC Company had the following information relating to the products sold during 2018.

| | |
|---|---|
| Total sales | $800,000 |
| Units sold | 6,400 units |
| Expected % of the products sold having defects | |
| Having no defect | 91% |
| Having minor defect | 6% |
| Having major defect | 3% |
| Estimated warranty cost per unit | |
| Minor defects | $ 7 |
| Major defects | $15 |

Compute the amount of warranty provision as at 31 December 2018. Ignore the effect of the time value of money.

① $ 2,688
② $ 2,880
③ $ 5,568
④ $24,000
⑤ $48,000

第37回 試験問題

Questions **31** and **32** are based on the following:

On 12 November 2018, XYZ Company made an agreement with a customer to supply 10,000 units of merchandise at a price of €140 per unit. The delivery date was 11 January 2019.

The following information was available relating to the merchandise as at 31 December 2018.

- XYZ Company held 8,000 units at a cost of €120 per unit and the estimated cost to sell the merchandise was €23 per unit.
- The unavoidable cost, including the estimated cost to sell, to deliver remaining 2,000 units was €147 per unit.

**31** What amount of write-down of the merchandise should XYZ Company recognise in accordance with IAS 2 for the year ended 31 December 2018?

1. €0
2. €24,000
3. €30,000
4. €32,000
5. €38,000

**32** What amount of provision in relation to the agreement should XYZ Company recognise in accordance with IAS 37 as at 31 December 2018?

1. €0
2. € 8,000
3. €14,000
4. €38,000
5. €80,000

283

第37回 試験問題

Questions 33 and 34 are based on the following:

ABC Company issued 40,000 no-par shares for cash at $20 per share. Subsequently, it repurchased 3,000 shares with cash at $32 per share and resold 1,500 shares at $30 per share.

33 Select the most appropriate number to fill in the following blank.

ABC Company paid for registration, legal and printing as the costs which were directly related to the issuance of the shares. These costs should be [          ].

① Capitalised as a deferred asset
② Deducted from equity
③ Expensed as an administrative cost
④ Recognised as a provision
⑤ Recognised in other comprehensive income

34 Which of the following journal entries should ABC Company make at the resale of 1,500 shares?

| ① Dr Cash | 45,000 | |
| Cr Share premium—treasury | | 45,000 |
| ② Dr Cash | 45,000 | |
| Cr Treasury shares | | 45,000 |
| ③ Dr Cash | 45,000 | |
| Cr Treasury shares | | 30,000 |
| Share premium—treasury | | 15,000 |
| ④ Dr Cash | 45,000 | |
| Loss on sale of treasury shares | 3,000 | |
| Cr Treasury shares | | 48,000 |
| ⑤ Dr Cash | 45,000 | |
| Share premium—treasury | 3,000 | |
| Cr Treasury shares | | 48,000 |

第37回 試験問題

35 On 1 January 2019, XYZ Company sold merchandise costing €7,200 to a customer for €24,200 and delivered the merchandise on the same date. Consideration for the contract is scheduled to be paid on 31 December 2020.

Additional information is as follows:

- The cash selling price of the merchandise was €20,000 on 1 January 2019.
- The contract includes a significant financing component.
- XYZ Company's right to the consideration is not conditioned on anything other than the passage of time.

What amount should XYZ Company recognise as revenue from the contract on 1 January 2019?

① € 7,200
② €12,800
③ €17,000
④ €20,000
⑤ €24,200


36 ABC Company sells Product A, Product B and Product C for $51,000. Stand-alone selling prices are as follows.

| | |
|---|---|
| Product A | $24,000 |
| Product B | 21,600 |
| Product C | 14,400 |

Additional information is as follows:

- ABC Company regularly sells Product A for $24,000.
- ABC Company regularly sells Product B and Product C together for $27,000.
- ABC Company has an observable evidence that the entire discount belongs to Product B and Product C.
- Product A, Product B and Product C are distinct performance obligations.

What amount of the selling price should be allocated to Product B?

① $16,200
② $18,360
③ $21,600
④ $27,000
⑤ $30,600

285

第37回 試験問題

Questions **37** and **38** are based on the following:

On 1 January 2018, XYZ Company entered into a 3-year contract to construct a commercial building for a customer for promised consideration of €4,000,000.

The following data are available relating to the construction for the year ended 31 December 2018.

| | |
|---|---|
| Estimated total costs to complete as at 1 January 2018 | €3,200,000 |
| Costs incurred during 2018 | 1,280,000 |
| Progress billing during 2018 | 1,560,000 |
| Cash collection during 2018 | 1,400,000 |

On 1 January 2019, XYZ Company and the customer agreed to modify the contract. As a result of the agreement, the promised consideration and estimated total costs increased by €1,100,000 and €800,000, respectively.

Additional information is as follows:

- XYZ Company accounts for the bundle of goods and services in the contract as a single performance obligation which is satisfied over time in accordance with IFRS 15.
- XYZ Company uses the input method based on costs incurred to measure its progress towards complete satisfaction of the performance obligation.
- On 1 January 2019, XYZ Company assessed the contract modification and concluded that the remaining goods and services are not distinct from the goods and services transferred on or before the date.
- The contract does not include any significant financing component.

**37** What amount should XYZ Company recognise as gross profit for the year ended 31 December 2018?

① € 120,000
② € 280,000
③ € 320,000
④ €1,400,000
⑤ €1,600,000

**38** As a result of the contract modification, what amount of additional revenue should XYZ Company recognise on 1 January 2019?

① €0
② € 30,000
③ € 32,000
④ € 440,000
⑤ €1,100,000

286

**39** On 1 February 2019, ABC Company sold merchandise to a customer with an assurance-type warranty for 1 year. In the sales contract, it also provided the customer with an optional extended warranty which adds an additional coverage for 3 years to the assurance-type warranty. ABC Company determined that the optional extended warranty is a distinct performance obligation.

Additional information is as follows:

- ABC Company received $5,600 cash for the sales contract from the customer on 1 February 2019.
- The stand-alone selling prices of the merchandise with an assurance-type warranty and the optional extended warranty were $5,850 and $150, respectively.
- The best estimate amount for the cost of the assurance-type warranty was $40.
- The assurance-type warranty only provides the customer with assurance that the merchandise complies with agreed-upon specifications.
- ABC Company had no observable evidence that the entire discount belonged to only one or two performance obligations.

What amount of revenue should ABC Company recognise from the performance obligation to transfer the merchandise on 1 February 2019?

① $5,410
② $5,420
③ $5,460
④ $5,600
⑤ $5,850

**40** On 1 November 2018, Company X received merchandise costing €13,000 on consignment from Company Y. During 2018, Company X sold half of the merchandise for €18,000 as an agent of Company Y. On 31 December 2018, Company X notified Company Y of the sales and remitted the cash due to Company Y after 10% of commission.

Under IFRS 15, what amount should Company X recognise as revenue from the sales of the merchandise for the year ended 31 December 2018?

① €  1,800
② €  9,700
③ €11,500
④ €16,200
⑤ €18,000

第37回 試験問題

**41** ABC Company has 700 employees and each employee is entitled to 15 days of paid annual leave for each year. Unused rights to the paid annual leave are carried over solely to the next year. The paid annual leave is taken on a last-in, first-out (LIFO) basis.

On 31 December 2018, the following information relating to the paid annual leave was available.

| | |
|---|---:|
| Carried-over annual leave to 2019 | 600 days |
| Expected usage of paid annual leave during 2019 | 11,000 days |
| Expected average salary of an employee per day in 2019 | $120 |

As at 31 December 2018, none of the employees was assumed to leave during 2019.

What amount of liability should ABC Company accrue in its statement of financial position as at 31 December 2018?

① $　　60,000
② $　　72,000
③ $　132,000
④ $1,260,000
⑤ $1,320,000

**42** On 1 January 2018, XYZ Company granted employees 5,000 share options to purchase XYZ Company's ordinary shares at €20 per share. These options vested on 1 January 2018.

The following information relates to the fair value of the ordinary shares and share options.

| | 1 January 2018 | 31 December 2018 |
|---|:---:|:---:|
| The fair value of each ordinary share | €17 | €24 |
| The fair value of each share option | 6 | 8 |

What amount of increase in equity should XYZ Company recognise for the year ended 31 December 2018?

① €　 30,000
② €　 40,000
③ €　 75,000
④ €100,000
⑤ €110,000

288

第37回 試験問題

Questions 🉤 through 🉥 are based on the following:

XYZ Company was founded at 1 January 2017 and recorded the following items for its statement of profit or loss.

|  | 2017 | 2018 |
|---|---|---|
| Sales | €54,000 | €78,000 |
| Expenses and losses excluding depreciation expense | 31,000 | 40,000 |
| Depreciation expense (*) | 10,000 | 10,000 |

(*) XYZ Company uses a different depreciation method for tax purposes. The table below indicates the book base and tax base of depreciable assets at the end of each year. The acquisition cost of the assets was €40,000.

|  | 2017 | 2018 | 2019 | 2020 |
|---|---|---|---|---|
| Book base | €30,000 | €20,000 | €10,000 | €0 |
| Tax base | 22,000 | 9,000 | 3,000 | 0 |

The enacted tax rate is 30% for 2017 and thereafter.

🉤 What amount of current income tax expense should XYZ Company report in its statement of profit or loss for the year ended 31 December 2017?

① €1,500
② €2,400
③ €3,900
④ €6,900
⑤ €7,200

🉥 What amount of profit should XYZ Company report in its statement of profit or loss for the year ended 31 December 2017?

① € 1,100
② € 9,100
③ €10,600
④ €11,500
⑤ €13,000

289

**45** What amount of deferred tax liability should XYZ Company report in its statement of financial position as at 31 December 2018?

① € 900
② €2,100
③ €2,400
④ €3,000
⑤ €3,300

**46** ABC Company made the following journal entry to record deferred tax asset due to $76,000 of a deductible temporary difference. The enacted tax rate was 20%.

Dr Deferred tax asset          15,200
    Cr Income tax expense—deferred        15,200

Subsequently, ABC Company determined that only 70% of the deferred tax asset was recoverable and made the following journal entry.

Dr [           ]     [   B   ]
  Cr [    A    ]         [        ]

Select the most appropriate combination to fill in A and B.

| | A | B |
|---|---|---|
| ① | Allowance to reduce deferred tax asset | 4,560 |
| ② | Allowance to reduce deferred tax asset | 10,640 |
| ③ | Deferred tax asset | 4,560 |
| ④ | Deferred tax asset | 10,640 |
| ⑤ | Income tax expense—deferred | 15,200 |

**47** ABC Company issued straight bonds and ordinary shares. It paid interest on the bonds and cash dividends on the shares.

As which activities may ABC Company classify the interest and dividends in its statement of cash flows?

| | Interest | Dividends |
|---|---|---|
| ① | Financing activities | Investing activities |
| ② | Investing activities | Financing activities |
| ③ | Investing activities | Operating activities |
| ④ | Operating activities | Investing activities |
| ⑤ | Operating activities | Operating activities |

第37回 試験問題

**48** XYZ Company purchased the following equity instruments.

| | |
|---|---|
| 1% of Company A's ordinary shares | €50,000 |
| 3% of Company B's ordinary shares | 40,000 |
| 20% of Company C's preference shares | 35,000 |
| 5% of XYZ Company's ordinary shares (treasury shares) | 73,000 |

Company A's ordinary shares are held for trading purposes and the others are not.

What amount should be net cash used in investing activities in XYZ Company's statement of cash flows?

① € 35,000
② € 75,000
③ € 85,000
④ €125,000
⑤ €148,000

過去問題

**49** ABC Company, preparing its statement of cash flows by the indirect method, had the following account balances.

| | 31 December 2017 | 31 December 2018 |
|---|---|---|
| Accounts receivable | $73,000 | $92,000 |
| Accounts payable | 77,000 | 81,000 |
| Inventory | 65,000 | 98,000 |

By what amount did net cash increase or decrease from the changes in the account balances?

① Decreased by $48,000.
② Decreased by $56,000.
③ Increased by $48,000.
④ Increased by $56,000.
⑤ No effect

**291**

第37回 試験問題

Questions **50** and **51** are based on the following:

At 1 January 2018, XYZ Company acquired 25% of another company's ordinary shares for €450,000 when the acquiree's fair value of net assets was the same as its book value, €900,000. The acquiree recorded €100,000 of profit for the year ended 31 December 2018 and declared and paid €40,000 of cash dividends during 2018.

Goodwill was not impaired as at 31 December 2018.

XYZ Company accounts for the acquiree's shares under the equity method.

**50** Which of the following journal entries should XYZ Company make to record the acquiree's cash dividends?

| | | | |
|---|---|---|---|
| ① Dr Cash | | 10,000 | |
| | Cr Dividends income | | 10,000 |
| ② Dr Cash | | 10,000 | |
| | Cr Investment | | 10,000 |
| ③ Dr Cash | | 10,000 | |
| | Non-controlling interest | 30,000 | |
| | Cr Investment | | 40,000 |
| ④ Dr Cash | | 40,000 | |
| | Cr Dividends income | | 10,000 |
| | Non-controlling interest | | 30,000 |
| ⑤ No journal entry is necessary. | | | |

**51** What amount of investment in the acquiree should XYZ Company report as at 31 December 2018?

① €147,500
② €240,000
③ €285,000
④ €465,000
⑤ €485,000

第37回 試験問題

Questions 52 and 53 are based on the following:

At 14 April 2016, ABC Company sold land, whose book value was $90,000, to its 60%-owned subsidiary for $110,000 cash. At 8 May 2018, the subsidiary sold the land to a third party for $120,000 cash.

Both ABC Company and the subsidiary account for the land using the cost model.

Respective financial statements of ABC Company and the subsidiary appropriately reflect the above transactions. ABC Company accounts for its investment in subsidiaries under the cost method.

52 Which of the following journal entries should ABC Company make in consolidation process for 2017?

① Dr Gain on sale of land        20,000
    Cr Land                           20,000

② Dr Land                       20,000
    Cr Gain on sale of land            20,000

③ Dr Land                       20,000
    Cr Retained earnings—beginning    20,000

④ Dr Retained earnings—beginning    20,000
    Cr Land                           20,000

⑤ No journal entry is necessary.

53 Which of the following journal entries should ABC Company make in consolidation process for 2018?

① Dr Gain on sale of land        10,000
    Cr Land                           10,000

② Dr Land                       10,000
    Cr Retained earnings—beginning    10,000

③ Dr Retained earnings—beginning    20,000
    Cr Gain on sale of land            20,000

④ Dr Retained earnings—beginning    20,000
    Cr Land                           20,000

⑤ No journal entry is necessary.

293

# 第37回 試験問題

**54** Company S, JPN Company's 80%-owned subsidiary, reported ¥580,000 of profit for the year ended 31 December 2018.

Company S's sales included ¥500,000 of sales of merchandise to JPN Company. JPN Company owned all the merchandise at the year-end. There was no other intercompany transaction. Company S's gross profit margin was 30%.

Compute Company S's profit attributable to non-controlling interests in JPN Company's consolidated statement of profit or loss for the year ended 31 December 2018.

    ① ¥16,000
    ② ¥46,000
    ③ ¥70,000
    ④ ¥80,000
    ⑤ ¥86,000


**55** At 1 January 2017, XYZ Company purchased a machine at a cost of €70,000 to which the cost model was applied. The residual value and the useful life were estimated at €7,000 and 6 years, respectively. At 1 January 2018, XYZ Company re-estimated that the useful life of the machine was 3 years from the date of acquisition and that the residual value was €4,000. XYZ Company used the straight-line method to compute depreciation expense.

What amount of depreciation expense should XYZ Company report in its statement of profit or loss for the year ended 31 December 2018?

    ① €10,500
    ② €22,000
    ③ €27,750
    ④ €33,000
    ⑤ €33,500


**56** The following information relates to JPN Company's ordinary shares.

- 10,000 shares were outstanding at 1 January.
- 4,000 additional shares were issued for cash at 1 July.
- 28,000 additional shares were issued as a result of a 3-for-1 share split at 1 October.

What is the number of ordinary shares to calculate earnings per share for the year?

    ① 14,000
    ② 19,000
    ③ 32,000
    ④ 36,000
    ⑤ 42,000

第37回 試験問題

Questions 57 and 58 are based on the following:

ABC Company has the following information to determine its earnings per share for the year ended 31 December 2018.

Ordinary shares
18,000 shares were outstanding from 1 January to 31 December.

Preference shares
5,000 of a $20 par value, 6% non-cumulative share were outstanding from 1 January to 31 December. ABC Company declared preference dividends during 2018.

Convertible bonds
ABC Company issued 2,000 convertible bonds at 1 January 2018. Each bond can be converted into one share anytime, and any one was not converted during 2018. $3,000 of interest expense was incurred for 2018 which arose from the liability component of the bonds. ABC Company's effective tax rate was 20% for 2018.

Profit for the year
$70,000

57 What amount should ABC Company report as basic earnings per share for the year ended 31 December 2018? If necessary, round off the amount to the second decimal place.

① $3.33
② $3.56
③ $3.89
④ $4.00
⑤ $6.74

58 What amount should ABC Company report as diluted earnings per share for the year ended 31 December 2018? If necessary, round off the amount to the second decimal place.

① $3.05
② $3.08
③ $3.20
④ $3.32
⑤ $3.38

第37回 試験問題

Questions 59 and 60 are based on the following:

The following information relates to JPN Company's operating segments.

|  |  |  | (Millions of yen) |  |
| --- | --- | --- | --- | --- |
| Segment | Sales to external customers | Intersegment sales | Operating profit | Assets |
| A | 831 | 34 | 76 | 667 |
| B | 772 | — | (14) | 603 |
| C | 552 | 80 | 29 | 319 |
| D | 479 | 22 | 10 | 491 |
| E | 201 | 16 | (13) | 227 |
| F | 108 | — | 3 | 50 |
|  | 2,943 | 152 | 91 | 2,357 |

59 Which segment meets the quantitative threshold of operating profit to be reported separately as a reportable segment?

    ① A and C
    ② A, B and C
    ③ A, C and D
    ④ A, B, C and D
    ⑤ A, B, C and E

60 How many reportable segments does JPN Company have?

    ① Two
    ② Three
    ③ Four
    ④ Five
    ⑤ Six

**61** XYZ Company was preparing its statement of profit or loss and other comprehensive income for the year ended 31 December 2018 and the following information was available temporarily.

| | |
|---|---|
| Revenue | €870,000 |
| Cost of sales | 620,000 |
| Selling, general and administrative expenses | 191,000 |
| Other income | 28,000 |
| Other expenses | 27,000 |
| Finance income | 8,000 |
| Finance costs | 19,000 |

The following items were not considered in the above information.

(a) Gain on sale of financial assets which were classified as measured at amortised cost, €13,000
(b) Gain on revaluation of land held for administrative purposes, €1,600*
(c) Loss on disposal of a component of XYZ Company, €15,000**
(d) Loss on translating foreign operations, €12,000***
(e) Volume discount incentives payable to customers, €5,000****

* XYZ Company uses the revaluation model for land. The credit balance in the revaluation surplus in respect of the land was €2,600 as at 1 January 2018.
** In addition to the loss on disposal, the component had net sales of €22,000, cost of sales of €11,000 and selling, general and administrative expenses of €14,000, all of which were not included in the above information.
*** The financial statements of the foreign operations were translated into the Euro. The foreign operations were not disposed of as at 31 December 2018. Income and expenses relating to the foreign operations were included in the above information.
**** All the volume discount incentives arose during 2018. It was highly probable that a significant reversal of revenue relating to the volume discount incentives would not occur.

Additional information is as follows:
- All the amounts above are shown before income taxes.
- Income tax rate for 2018 was 25%.
- All the differences between taxable income or loss and pre-tax financial income or loss, which arose from items recorded in other comprehensive income, were temporary.
- The deferred tax assets were expected to be recovered in the future period.
- XYZ Company prepares the statement of profit or loss and other comprehensive income in two statements with expenses classified by function.

第37回 試験問題

(1) Complete the following statement of profit or loss. If necessary, enclose negative numbers in parentheses (e.g. × − 230 → ○ (230)).

XYZ Company
Statement of Profit or Loss
For the Year Ended 31 December 2018

(Unit: €)

| | |
|---|---:|
| Revenue | [          ] |
| Cost of sales | (620,000) |
| Gross profit | [          ] |
| Selling, general and administrative expenses | (191,000) |
| Other income | 28,000 |
| Other expenses | [          ] |
| Finance income | [          ] |
| Finance costs | (19,000) |
| Profit before tax | [          ] |
| Income tax expense | [          ] |
| Profit for the year from continuing operations | [          ] |
| Loss for the year from discontinued operations, net of tax | [          ] |
| Profit for the year | [          ] |

(2) Calculate the following amounts. If necessary, enclose negative numbers in parentheses (e.g. × − 230 → ○ (230)).

(A) Components of other comprehensive income that will not be reclassified to profit or loss, net of tax € [          ]

(B) Components of other comprehensive income that may be reclassified to profit or loss, net of tax € [          ]

(C) Total comprehensive income for the year € [          ]

第37回 試験問題

62 The following information relates to ABC Company's defined benefit pension plan.

| | |
|---|---|
| On 31 December 2017: | |
| Present value of defined benefit obligation | $630,000 |
| Fair value of plan assets | 610,000 |
| | |
| During 2018: | |
| Current service cost | $ 22,000 |
| Past service cost* | 17,000 |
| Return on plan assets | 32,000 |
| Contributions | 34,000 |
| Benefit paid | 19,000 |
| | |
| On 31 December 2018: | |
| Present value of defined benefit obligation | $688,350 |
| Fair value of plan assets | 657,000 |
| | |
| Actuarial loss** | 6,000 |
| Return on plan assets excluding the interest income on plan assets | ? |
| | |
| Discount rate | 5% |

* The past service cost arose, because the pension plan was amended on 1 January 2018.

**The actuarial loss arose, because some actuarial assumptions were amended at the end of 2018. It is included in the present value of defined benefit obligation on 31 December 2018.

There was no accumulated other comprehensive income relating to the remeasurements of the net defined benefit liability as at 31 December 2017.

299

(1) Calculate the return on plan assets excluding the interest income on plan assets on 31 December 2018. If necessary, enclose negative numbers in parentheses (e.g. × − 230 → ○ (230)).

$[          ]

(2) Complete the following reconciliation of the present value of defined benefit obligation. Select the appropriate numbers for ⌷⌷⌷⌷⌷⌷⌷ from the list below and enter the amounts for [          ]. If necessary, enclose negative numbers in parentheses (e.g. × − 230 → ○ (230)).

| 1. Benefit paid | 2. Contributions | 3. Current service cost |
| 4. Interest cost | 5. Interest income | 6. Return on plan assets |

Reconciliation of present value of defined benefit obligation
from 31 December 2017 to 31 December 2018

| Beginning balance as at 31 December 2017 | | $630,000 |
| Past service cost | | 17,000 |
| ⌷⌷⌷⌷⌷⌷ | [          ] |
| ⌷⌷⌷⌷⌷⌷ | [          ] |
| ⌷⌷⌷⌷⌷⌷ | [          ] |
| Actuarial loss | | 6,000 |
| Ending balance as at 31 December 2018 | | $688,350 |

(3) What amount of the net defined benefit liability or asset should ABC Company report in its statement of financial position as at 31 December 2018?

$[          ] of ( Liability   Asset ) (Circle the right answer.)

(4) What amount should ABC Company recognise in profit or loss relating to the net defined benefit liability or asset for the year ended 31 December 2018?

$[          ] of ( Expense   Income ) (Circle the right answer.)

(5) What amount of the remeasurements of the net defined benefit liability or asset should be debited or credited to other comprehensive income for the year ended 31 December 2018?

$[          ] of ( Debit   Credit ) (Circle the right answer.)

第37回 試験問題

63 At 30 June 2019, P Company acquired a 60% share of S Company for €97,000 cash and obtained control of S Company. Immediately before the acquisition, the statements of financial position of both companies were as follows:

P Company

| Cash | €162,000 | Trade and other payables | € 80,000 |
|---|---|---|---|
| Trade and other receivables | 65,000 | Share capital | 200,000 |
| Inventory | 143,000 | Share premium | 300,000 |
| Property, plant and equipment | 626,000 | Retained earnings | 416,000 |
| | €996,000 | | €996,000 |

S Company

| Cash | € 24,000 | Trade and other payables | € 35,000 |
|---|---|---|---|
| Trade and other receivables | 17,000 | Share capital | 40,000 |
| Inventory* | 21,000 | Share premium | 10,000 |
| Property, plant and equipment* | 86,000 | Retained earnings | 63,000 |
| | €148,000 | | €148,000 |

*The fair values of inventory and property, plant and equipment were €30,000 and €90,000, respectively.

The fair value of non-controlling interest was €58,000 and P Company chose to measure the non-controlling interest in S Company at fair value.

(1) Complete P Company's consolidated statement of financial position immediately after acquisition. Select the appropriate numbers for [_____] from the list below and enter the amounts for [          ].

| 1 Investment in S Company | 4 Other component of equity |
|---|---|
| 2 Goodwill | 5 Other current assets |
| 3 Non-controlling interest | 6 Other intangible assets |

P Company's Consolidated Statement of Financial Position

| Cash | €[        ] | Trade and other payables | €[        ] |
|---|---|---|---|
| Trade and other receivables | [        ] | Share capital | [        ] |
| Inventory | [        ] | Share premium | [        ] |
| Property, plant and equipment | [        ] | Retained earnings | [        ] |
| | [        ] | | [        ] |
| | €[        ] | | €[        ] |

(2) Assume that P Company chose to measure the non-controlling interest in S Company at the non-controlling interest's proportionate share of S Company's identifiable net assets. Calculate the following amounts in P Company's consolidated statement of financial position immediately after acquisition.

(A) Non-controlling interest     €[          ]
(B) Goodwill                     €[          ]

301

## 第37回 試験問題

64 An Australian subsidiary of a Japanese company was established on 1 January 2018 by issuing shares for $70,000 cash. The subsidiary's functional currency is the Austrian dollar and its presentation currency is the Japanese yen.

The subsidiary's financial statements in dollars are as follows:

| Statement of Financial Position As at 31 December 2018 | | | |
|---|---|---|---|
| **Assets** | | **Equity** | |
| Cash | $39,000 | Share capital (*2) | $70,000 |
| Land (*1) | 37,000 | Retained earnings | 6,000 |
| | $76,000 | | $76,000 |

| Statement of Profit or Loss For the Year Ended 31 December 2018 | |
|---|---|
| Revenue (*3) | $30,000 |
| Expenses (*4) | 24,000 |
| Profit | $ 6,000 |

(*1) Land was purchased with cash at 12 March. Management chose to measure it at cost.

(*2) Management chose to translate share capital using the exchange rate at the date of the transaction.

(*3) A service was performed for $10,000 cash at 8 August, and another service was performed for $20,000 cash at 23 October.

(*4) Expenses were incurred and paid on 15 February.

Exchange rates were as follows:

| Date | Exchange rate |
|---|---|
| 1 January | $1 = ¥88 |
| 15 February | $1 = ¥85 |
| 12 March | $1 = ¥82 |
| 8 August | $1 = ¥81 |
| 23 October | $1 = ¥80 |
| 31 December | $1 = ¥78 |
| Weighted average for 2018 | $1 = ¥83 |

Complete the subsidiary's statements of financial position and profit or loss in yen by entering the appropriate amounts for each [                    ]. Its statement of other comprehensive income is omitted. Enclose negative numbers in parentheses. If a field is not used, fill in with "—" (dash).

| Statement of Financial Position As at 31 December 2018 | | | |
|---|---|---|---|
| **Assets** | | **Equity** | |
| Cash ¥[        ] | | Share capital        ¥[        ] | |
| Land   [        ] | | Retained earnings  [        ] | |
| | | Other component of equity        [        ] | |
| ¥[        ] | | ¥[        ] | |

| Statement of Profit or Loss For the Year Ended 31 December 2018 | |
|---|---|
| Revenue | ¥[        ] |
| Expenses | [        ] |
| Foreign exchange translation gain (loss) | [        ] |
| Profit (Loss) | ¥[        ] |

302

## 第37回 試験問題

# 模範解答

**1~60**（各7点　計420点）

| | | | | | | | | | | | | |
|---|---|---|---|---|---|---|---|---|---|---|---|---|
| | | | | | | Subject2 | | | | | | |
| 問 | 解答 | 問 | 解答 | 問 | 解答 | 問 | 解答 | 問 | 解答 | 問 | 解答 |
| 1 | ② | 11 | ① | 21 | ⑤ | 31 | ② | 41 | ① | 51 | ④ |
| 2 | ① | 12 | ② | 22 | ③ | 32 | ③ | 42 | ① | 52 | ④ |
| 3 | ③ | 13 | ④ | 23 | ④ | 33 | ② | 43 | ① | 53 | ③ |
| 4 | ④ | 14 | ④ | 24 | ③ | 34 | ⑤ | 44 | ② | 54 | ⑤ |
| 5 | ④ | 15 | ② | 25 | ④ | 35 | ④ | 45 | ⑤ | 55 | ③ |
| 6 | ④ | 16 | ② | 26 | ③ | 36 | ① | 46 | ③ | 56 | ④ |
| 7 | ③ | 17 | ① | 27 | ② | 37 | ③ | 47 | ⑤ | 57 | ② |
| 8 | ② | 18 | ④ | 28 | ① | 38 | ③ | 48 | ② | 58 | ④ |
| 9 | ③ | 19 | ③ | 29 | ① | 39 | ③ | 49 | ① | 59 | ⑤ |
| 10 | ② | 20 | ④ | 30 | ③ | 40 | ① | 50 | ② | 60 | ④ |

**61**（45点）

(1)

XYZ Company
Statement of Profit or Loss
For the Year Ended 31 December 2018

(Unit：€)

| | |
|---|---|
| Revenue | [　865,000　] |
| Cost of sales | (620,000) |
| Gross profit | [　245,000　] |
| Selling, general and administrative expenses | (191,000) |
| Other income | 28,000 |
| Other expenses | [　(27,000)　] |
| Finance income | [　21,000　] |
| Finance costs | (19,000) |
| Profit before tax | [　57,000　] |
| Income tax expense | [　(14,250)　] |
| Profit for the year from continuing operations | [　42,750　] |
| Loss for the year from discontinued operations, net of tax | [　(13,500)　] |
| Profit for the year | [　29,250　] |

(2)

(A) €［　　1,200　　］
(B) €［　（9,000）　］
(C) €［　21,450　　］

303

第37回 試験問題

## 62 (45点)

(1)  $ [    1,500    ]

(2)

Reconciliation of present value of defined benefit obligation
from 31 December 2017 to 31 December 2018

| Beginning balance as at 31 December 2017 | | $630,000 |
|---|---|---|
| Past service cost | | 17,000 |
| 3 | [    22,000    ] | |
| 4 | [    32,350    ] | 順不同 |
| 1 | [   (19,000)   ] | |
| Actuarial loss | | 6,000 |
| Ending balance as at 31 December 2018 | | $688,350 |

(3)  $ [    31,350    ] of ( ⟨Liability⟩    Asset    )
(4)  $ [    40,850    ] of ( ⟨Expense⟩    Income    )
(5)  $ [     4,500    ] of ( ⟨Debit⟩    Credit    )

## 63 (45点)

(1)

P Company's Consolidated Statement of Financial Position

| Cash | €[    89,000    ] | Trade and other payables | €[    115,000    ] |
|---|---|---|---|
| Trade and other receivables | [    82,000    ] | Share capital | [    200,000    ] |
| Inventory | [    173,000    ] | Share premium | [    300,000    ] |
| Property, plant and equipment | [    716,000    ] | Retained earnings | [    416,000    ] |
| 2 | [    29,000    ] | 3 | [    58,000    ] |
| | €[  1,089,000  ] | | €[  1,089,000  ] |

(2)

(A) €[    50,400    ]

(B) €[    21,400    ]

304

**64** （45点）

```
                        Statement of Financial Position
                            As at 31 December 2018

            Assets                                    Equity

Cash      ¥[   3,042,000  ]     Share capital         ¥[   6,160,000  ]

Land      [   2,886,000  ]     Retained earnings      [     370,000  ]

                               Other component of equity  [   (602,000)  ]

          ¥[   5,928,000  ]                           ¥[   5,928,000  ]
```

```
                        Statement of Profit or Loss
                    For the Year Ended 31 December 2018

Revenue                                ¥[   2,410,000  ]

Expenses                               [  (2,040,000)  ]

Foreign exchange translation gain(loss)  [      —       ]

Profit(Loss)                           ¥[     370,000  ]
```

305

2019年1月1日現在の基準書・解釈指針を収める
**IFRS財団公認日本語版！**

# IFRS®基準〈注釈付き〉2019

IFRS財団 編　企業会計基準委員会　監訳
　　　　　　　公益財団法人 財務会計基準機構

中央経済社刊　定価19,800円（分売はしておりません）B5判・4752頁
ISBN978-4-502-32051-4

## IFRS適用に必備の書！

●**唯一の公式日本語訳・最新版**　本書はIFRSの基準書全文の唯一の公式日本語訳。2019年版から、IFRS導入に向けた準備・学習にも役立つ〈注釈付き〉に衣更え。具体的には、基準間の相互参照で、関連規定が検索しやすくなり、さらに、実務論点の宝庫であるIFRS解釈指針委員会のアジェンダ決定も豊富に収録している。

●**使いやすい3分冊**　2018年版から英語版の原書が3分冊となったため、日本語版もPART A・PART B・PART Cの3分冊の刊行となっている。「要求事項」、「概念フレームワーク」をPART Aに、「付属ガイダンス」、「実務記述書」をPART Bに、「結論の根拠」をPART Cに収録している。

●**新規掲載項目**　改訂「財務報告に関する概念フレームワーク」（2018年3月公表）、「『重要性がある』の定義」（IAS第1号及びIAS第8号の修正）など、最新基準等を収録。

IFRSの参照に当たっては、つねに最新の日本語版をご覧ください。

中央経済社
東京・神田神保町1
電話 03-3293-3381
FAX 03-3291-4437
http://www.chuokeizai.co.jp/

収録内容
基準書本文
（基準・適用指針）
財務報告に関する
概念フレームワーク
　　　　　　PART A収録
適用ガイダンス・設例
IFRS実務記述書
　　　　　　PART B収録
結論の根拠　PART C収録

▶価格は税込みです。掲載書籍は中央経済社ホームページ http://www.chuokeizai.co.jp/ からもお求めいただけます。

## BATIC企画委員会 (敬称略・順不同)

| 委員長 | 平松 | 一夫 |
|--------|------|------|
| 委員 | 井上 | 達男 |
| 委員 | 樋口 | 哲朗 |
| 委員 | 秋葉 | 賢一 |
| 委員 | 田宮 | 治雄 |
| 委員 | 乂邊 | 崇 |

---

＜IFRSからの引用箇所について＞

本テキストにはIFRS財団がすべての権利を保有する著作物が含まれている。東京商工会議所による複製はIFRS財団の許諾を得ている。第三者への複製・配布を禁ず。IFRS基準書及びIFRS財団の著作物に関する情報はhttp://eifrs.ifrs.orgまで。

IASB、IFRS財団、著者者、および発行者は、この著作中の内容に依拠して活動すること、または活動をしないことによって生じたいかなる損失についても何ら責任を負わない。その損失が、過失、またはそれ以外によって生じたかどうかは問わない。

This publication contains copyright material of the IFRS Foundation in respect of which all rights are reserved. Reproduced by the Tokyo Chamber of Commerce and Industry with the permission of the IFRS Foundation. No permission granted to third parties to reproduce or distribute. For full access to IFRS Standards and the work of the IFRS Foundation please visit http://eifrs.ifrs.org

The International Accounting Standards Board, the IFRS Foundation, the authors and the publishers do not accept responsibility for any loss caused by acting or refraining from acting in reliance on the material in this publication, whether such loss is caused by negligence or otherwise.

---

## BATIC® Subject 2 公式問題集 (2020年版)
### Accounting Manager & Controller Level

2020年 3月31日 初版第1刷発行

| | | |
|--|--|--|
| 編　集 | 東京商工会議所 |
| 発行者 | 小林 治彦 |
| 発行所 | 東京商工会議所 |
| | 検定センター |
| | 〒100-0005　東京都千代田区丸の内3-2-2 |
| | （丸の内二重橋ビル） |
| | TEL (03) 3989-0777 |
| 協　力 | (株) イーストゲート |
| 発売元 | (株) 中央経済グループパブリッシング |
| | 〒101-0051　東京都千代田区神田神保町1-31-2 |
| | TEL (03) 3293-3381 |
| | FAX (03) 3291-4437 |
| 印刷所 | こだま印刷(株) |

---

● 本書は著作権上の保護を受けています。本書の一部あるいは全部について東京商工会議所から文書による承諾を得ずに、いかなる方法においても無断で複写、複製することは禁じられています。

● 「BATIC (国際会計検定)」「BATIC」は東京商工会議所の商標登録です。

● テキストに関する最新情報はホームページ (https://www.kentei.org/) でご確認いただけます。

● 落丁、乱丁本は、送料発売元負担においてお取り替えいたします。

©2020　東京商工会議所　Printed in Japan
ISBN978-4-502-34041-3 C3034